# The Baby Snatchers

# The Baby Snatchers

A young mother's desperate fight to escape the
Sacred Heart nuns and keep her baby

## MARY CREIGHTON

### WITH VERONICA CLARK

BLINK
bringing you closer

Published by Blink Publishing
3.08, The Plaza,
535 Kings Road,
Chelsea Harbour,
London, SW10 0SZ

www.blinkpublishing.co.uk

facebook.com/blinkpublishing
twitter.com/blinkpublishing

Paperback – 978-1-911-600-28-2
Ebook – 978-1-911-600-29-9

A CIP catalogue of this book is available from the British Library.

Typeset by seagulls.net
Printed and bound by Clays Ltd, St. Ives Plc

3 5 7 9 10 8 6 4

This book is a work of non-fiction, based on the life, experiences
and recollections of Mary Creighton. Certain details in this story,
including names, have been changed to protect identity and privacy.

Every reasonable effort has been made to trace copyright holders of
material reproduced in this book, but if any have been inadvertently
overlooked the publishers would be glad to hear from them.

Blink Publishing is an imprint of the Bonnier Publishing Group
www.bonnierpublishing.co.uk

# Contents

# Prologue

Carefully choosing the horseshoe nail, the old workman studies it closely, rolling it over in his grimy palm. Reverently, he rubs its rust against the sleeve of his filthy and tattered jacket, dusty with the toil of a humble labourer. Placing the nail between the thumb and forefinger of his calloused left hand, he carefully traces the wall, trying to find a suitable resting place. Lifting the lump hammer, he rests the nail against the stone wall with a gentleness that belies his tough exterior and lowly social standing. The silence of the early morning dawn is shattered by the stark blow of the hammer, and another, and another...

BANG. BANG. BANG.

The sound reverberates across the grounds – a nail driven home in the same way of a crucifixion almost 2,000 years before.

Black crows caw and scatter instantly from the trees, cast out in the autumnal early morning mist.

His gentleness has gone, replaced instead by a surging anger. He shouldn't have to do this.

The hammer blows cease abruptly as he hears the sound of the latch, and then the rustle of the leaves as the wooden door creaks open, pushing them aside. Then he sees her from the corner of his eye. The nun sweeps by imperiously and passes the elderly workman without a second glance. She thinks he is beneath her in class, intellect, and strength of faith. As her black robes swish past, the labourer clenches his hand around the hammer. His knuckles flash white with anger as he grips the handle in disgust. The nun glances back and he removes his cloth cap. She thinks it is a belated mark of respect for her. It is anything but.

The significance of the horseshoe nails remains the workman's secret for decades. Nobody notices them as they multiply and spread across the crumbling convent wall over the years that follow. Each humble nail embodies a terrible truth that will only be revealed over half a century later, and one that will become Ireland's greatest shame.

# CHAPTER 1

# Deadly Daffodils

'Come on, Mary. Hurry up!' One of the girls waved as she called over to me.

I tried my best to catch up with the rest of the group. I didn't want to be last because I knew all the best flowers would be gone. But the grass was long, and the blades caught against my legs, slowing me down. By now I felt breathless, but I was determined not to miss out. The grass continued to part as I crushed it underfoot, ploughing my way through the field. I was only five, but I was determined to keep up with the rest of the gang who were twice my age. It wasn't the first time we'd done this but, although I didn't realise it then, it would be my last.

Rural Ireland had never looked more beautiful as I dashed through the field without a care in the world. The sun shone high in the sky in the spring morning, and the day seemed endless as it stretched out in front of me. Jumping over a small ditch, I crossed the second field. That's when I spotted them all lined up in the distance. They were standing proudly, like a golden crown, atop a drystone wall where the field ended and his garden began. A garden full of beautiful daffodils the exact same colour as the sun. There were hundreds of them dotted across the landscape. I stopped momentarily to catch my breath and watched in wonder as their elegant green stems swayed gently in the breeze. The heavy yellow flowers nodded in time as though they were dancing to a silent tune.

'Mary, over here,' an older girl shouted over, her voice breaking my thoughts. She was standing beside the wall and smiled as she lifted her hand high into the air and beckoned me over.

I gambolled over towards her and the wall between the field and his garden. But the garden ran level on top of the wall, which was much too tall for me to scale. The girl realised and dipped down at the side of me. Slotting her fingers together, she formed a makeshift step with her hands.

'Here,' she gestured, holding it out for me to climb on to.

Placing an uncertain foot on it, I was lifted up and my bare legs scrambled against stone, my skin scratching against the wall as I shinned myself up and into his high garden.

'That's it, Mary!'

The girl wasn't just older but taller too, so she was able to clear the wall easily. Soon we'd found ourselves standing alongside the other children in Dr Gallagher's prized garden. I watched as the others knelt down and began to help themselves to the brightest and prettiest flowers I'd ever seen. I wanted an armful of daffodils to take home for my neighbours and Mum. She'd seemed so unhappy lately, and I desperately wanted to see her smile again. With my scraped knees against the warm earth, I began snapping the stems close to the ground. I wanted my flowers to be tall and elegant. An older boy nodded over in approval as I continued to pick my beautiful bouquet. I was so engrossed in what I was doing that I didn't notice him stand up and signal over towards the rest of the gang.

'Quick, old man Gallagher's here!'

Although I'd heard the words I was too busy concentrating on my flowers to take them in. A slight breeze rose and brushed against my skin as the other children stopped what they were doing and ran past me towards the wall and the safety of the field. By the time I glanced up I realised I was all alone, hidden among the flowers.

'Marrrryy!'

It was the girl, calling to me, warning me that trouble was on its way. I quickly scrambled to my feet, and, using the flat palms of my hands, wiped the mud from my knees. As I glanced over my shoulder I saw him – Dr Gallagher. He was running out of his house and over towards me. But all I could focus on was a shotgun hanging over the crook of his arm – metal, heavy and menacing.

'Mary, come on!' the others cried, urging me to run for my life.

The doctor shouted something, but I was so scared that blood was pumping inside my ears, drowning out his words. However, I could tell from the look on his face he'd recognised me. He knew I was part of the gang and that this wasn't the first time I'd stolen blooms from his garden.

'Come here, you vagabond!' I heard that all right as his booming voice carried loud and clear across the lawn.

I turned and ran as fast as my legs would carry me. I clutched my stolen bouquet as though my life depended upon it. The daffodil heads flapped and bobbed up and down as I sprinted away from the doctor and his gun. Suddenly, he broke into a run and began to give chase.

'I'll kill you if I catch you! This isn't the first time!' he roared.

I looked over towards the others. They were specks of colour in the distance, tearing halfway across the field with their arms bursting with shocks of yellow flowers.

'I'll kill the lot of yous!'

I kept on running, but soon I found it hard to breathe. Air burned inside my lungs, which felt as though they were on fire as I gasped for breath. I turned back. Dr Gallagher was old but he was extremely tall and thin, and his long legs seemed to cover twice as much ground as mine.

'Stop right now!'

But I had no intention of doing as he said. Instead, I kept on running. I turned once more and noticed that his face was beetroot. I wasn't sure if it was with anger or the sheer effort of running. Struggling for each breath, I darted as fast as I could towards the... and that's when

I remembered it – the wall. I realised I'd never clear it without help. My eyes scoured the adjoining field for the gang but they'd already fled, leaving me to my fate. I had to clear the wall; I was all alone and so I had no choice. Soon I'd reached it and the edge of Dr Gallagher's garden. Bits of soil crumbled beneath my feet and fell into the field below as I teetered along the edge of it. I contemplated the five-foot drop below me and took a large gulp of breath for courage. Closing my eyes, I leapt into thin air. My arms and legs flailed against a nothingness as the sensation of falling lifted my stomach up and into my mouth. With no one there to catch me, I landed hard against the solid ground with a sickening thump. The stolen flowers flew upwards into the air before scattering all around.

'Owww!' I whimpered as my arms and legs lay twisted beneath me.

The air had been knocked from my lungs. I'd been winded by the impact. I felt my shinbone throb as I opened my eyes and looked up at the blue sky. I knew I had to move because the doctor was coming, the doctor and his gun. I pulled myself up and looked at my leg. Tiny specks of blood had begun to ooze where the earth had grazed away the top layer of skin. Normally, I'd have been scared because I hated the sight of blood, but I didn't have time to feel frightened because Dr Gallagher was almost upon me. Gathering up the scattered daffodils as best I could, I clambered to my feet and crossed the field over towards the next one. The doctor stopped at the wall of his garden and watched as I limped pathetically across the field. Eventually I reached the safety of the ditch and the other children.

'Phew, that was close!' the boy said, his eyes wide with the drama of it all. He lifted a sleeve to his face and wiped his snotty nose against it. 'He's crazy, that old man Gallagher!'

The others nodded in agreement as the older girl stepped forward and over towards me.

'Are you all right, Mary?' she asked as she pointed down at my bloodied leg.

'Grand, I'm just grand,' I grinned. But I wasn't. My leg felt odd, almost dead, as though it'd somehow detached itself from the rest of my body.

Afterwards, me and the rest of the gang made our way up the lane and back towards the village. One by one, boys and girls, each one with an armful of stolen daffodils from the doctor's garden, peeled off into their houses. As soon as I limped in through the back door, my mother was waiting for me. I smiled, hoping she'd be delighted with the bouquet in my arms, but instead she was annoyed.

'And where'd you be getting those from?' she asked, eyeing them suspiciously.

'Up the lane… from a garden.'

I might be a flower thief, but I certainly wasn't a liar.

'What garden?' She took the blooms from my arms and stood them up inside a vase of cold water.

'The man's garden.'

'What man and what garden?'

I watched as her face twitched with doubt.

'The man up the road. The flowers grow wild in his garden.'

I decided not to mention that the man was a gentleman and a doctor to boot.

Mum tutted disapprovingly.

'I told you not to go up there but you—'

She stopped mid-sentence as she caught sight of my muddy legs.

'Look at the state of you, Mary Creighton!' she said, turning sharply. She headed over towards the sink and pulled out an old dishcloth.

'Sit on the stool,' she ordered, 'and don't move until I say so.'

I sat down on the small wooden stool and watched as she dipped a corner of the cloth in some lukewarm water and began to bathe my right leg. I could tell she was annoyed about the flowers. It was the way she roughly wiped the mud and grass stains from my legs. She was so heavy-handed that at one point I pulled away from her.

'Owww!'

'Well, hold still then! I can't do anything if you keep wriggling now, can I?'

I did as I was told. I knew better than to suffer Mum's unpredictable temper. Weirdly though, once she'd cleaned me up nothing more was said about the flowers. Instead, they took pride of place in the kitchen window – a constant reminder of the doctor and what I'd done.

I'd always been a daddy's girl, but he often worked away, leaving me under the care of my mother. While my father had adored me, my mother was cold, with a quick temper, and she barely tolerated me, ill or not.

The following morning I awoke early, but as I tried to climb out of bed my right leg remained on the mattress, as heavy and as dead as a lump of wood.

'Come on, you'll be late for school,' Mum nagged, popping her head around the door to try and hurry me up.

'It's my leg,' I explained. I pulled the blanket back to show her. 'I can't feel it.'

She pushed open the door and came bounding over towards me. I could tell her patience was beginning to wear thin.

'What's wrong with it? Does it hurt?' she asked, prodding it.

She waited for me to wince and pull away from her, but instead I felt nothing.

'No, I can't feel it.'

'Well, if there's no pain then there are no excuses. Up for school you get.'

Standing up, she wiped both hands against her apron and left the room.

I knew she'd make me go, so I got up and got dressed. It was awkward trying to walk with a dead leg, but somehow I managed to drag myself a whole mile to school. It took ages, but miraculously I made it just in time for the first bell. Back then, boys and girls were kept separate in the playground. The girls weren't usually rough, but after lunch when one girl pushed past she sent me reeling backwards. I managed to stay upright but the full weight on my deadened leg had somehow woken it back up – this time with a vengeance. A hot pain shot from my toes up to my knee, travelling the length and breadth of my shinbone. I felt as though my whole leg was on fire with pain.

'Arrrghhh!' I howled.

I was rooted to the spot as the burning white-hot pain radiated up and along my leg, causing my calf muscle to swell up. The other children didn't know what to do or what was wrong with me, and I couldn't tell them for yelling. My pitiful cries caught the ear of Sister Celestine, who came running over to see what all the fuss was about. Sister Celestine wasn't known for her compassion, and soon she was standing in front of me with a stern look upon her face. The black nun's habit she wore hung off her bony frame and flapped around in the breeze like a bat out of hell.

'What's wrong with you, child?' she demanded to know. Sister pursed her lips together in annoyance. 'And why are you making that awful racket?'

I attempted to answer, but hot tears were streaming down both cheeks as I tried, but failed, to hold the excruciating pain inside.

'Shut up, child! Shut up with you now!' Sister snapped.

She raised a bony finger and pointed over towards a queue that had formed in front of the person ringing the bell. 'Now go and get in line with the other girls.'

I hobbled over to join the rest of my class but the pain was intolerable.

'Mary Creighton, for goodness' sake, stand still and be quiet!' Sister barked as she moved down the queue and counted the children's heads one by one. 'Now go inside, children, and be quick about it!' she said, directing the last bit towards me.

I buried my face against my sleeve and sobbed silently into it. I didn't want to get into trouble, but I couldn't help myself – the pain was unbearable. Back inside the classroom, I watched as Sister pulled out a makeshift stage and told the class to climb up on to it.

'Choir practice!' she announced, clapping her hands together as though she was herding a flock of sheep.

My leg was still killing me and I couldn't climb up, which only served to infuriate her further.

'Very well,' she said in a voice that suggested she didn't believe a single word of it. 'You'll just have to sit down on the side, but for goodness' sake, stop your wailing. This is your final warning, Mary Creighton!'

I tried, but I couldn't stop. I continued to sob even when the class had begun to sing. Their voices soared high into the air – a beautiful noise pierced by the sound of my intermittent whimpers during the quieter parts. Sister Celestine was furious.

'Shut up, Mary Creighton, or I will strike you!' she said, raising a hand in final warning.

But I couldn't keep still or be quiet. Soon her fury had reached boiling point. She told the rest of the class to stay where they were and grabbed me roughly by the scruff of my neck. Then she unceremoniously dragged me to the front of the class, where she plucked the cane from against the wall. I screamed out in agony.

'Hold out your hand...'

I didn't move.

'I said, hold out your hand or you'll feel even worse, child.'

My fingers trembled before me as Sister raised the cane high behind her head and brought it crashing down against my palm. The cane sliced into the fleshier part, leaving a bright red welt where it had struck.

'I can't hear the choir for your crying!' she shouted as she continued to whip my hand harder and harder. Her temper increased with every swipe.

Once she'd finished I sat down at my desk for the rest of the day, my sobs finally giving in to an exhausted whimper. I remained like that for almost two hours until a little girl's father popped his head around the class door.

'I'm here to pick up Caitlin,' he told Sister, but as he spoke his eyes fell on me.

He was so shocked when he saw how distressed I was that he immediately offered to take me home in his car. Back then, it was unusual to have a car.

I looked up at Sister, who just seemed relieved to be rid of me early.

'Very well.'

I travelled home with my classmate in her father's car, but I couldn't stop crying.

'I don't know what's wrong with her,' he told my mother after we'd pulled up outside the house. 'She cried all the way home, and Sister Celestine says she's been crying all day.'

I wasn't a cry baby and Mum knew it. She realised something was seriously wrong and sent word to my father, who was working for a company up the road. Within minutes he was home. Lifting me gently up into his arms, he carried me over to his bicycle and balanced me across the crossbar. He climbed on and cycled over to Ballina village hospital. The doctors examined me but didn't have a clue what was wrong. Instead they admitted me and prescribed a strong course of antibiotics. I remained in hospital for a fortnight but my leg refused to heal. The initial graze had slowly blistered and turned into an open sore that oozed a disgusting yellow-green pus. My leg became badly infected and I had to have the wound dressed with fresh bandages four times a day to keep the flies away. The smell was so horrible that the other children refused to come near me. But still

I didn't heal. My education began to suffer as a result as one long spell in hospital followed another. I underwent a couple of operations but nothing seemed to work. The doctors were baffled and would crowd at the end of my bed, scratching their heads while referring to their medical journals. The hospital nurses continued to clean out my wound with a long, black cylindrical stick, which was the width of a pencil. I didn't know what it was, but it didn't work. The wound continued to weep until other identical sores broke out across the rest of my shin. The baffled doctors transferred me to Castlebar hospital for others to examine me. I didn't know then, but one of the doctors had spoken to Aunt Mary, my father's sister, explaining the only way to 'cure' me would be to amputate my leg. But Dad went berserk when Aunt Mary told him.

'Over my dead body! No one is going to butcher my daughter!'

With no improvement but with my condition stabilised, I returned home, albeit briefly. It was 1960, and my family had moved to a better house with running water and an inside toilet. I was particularly keen to see the inside toilet because back then it was considered the height of luxury. I remained on medication and had to attend regular check-ups, but no one could tell my parents what was wrong with me.

A few months later, Mum gave birth to another baby girl, although I didn't have the chance to get to know my new sister because I was transferred again, this time to a hospital in Galway, almost 70 miles away from home. It was at Dad's insistence that I'd been moved a third time.

'I refuse to stand by and watch my little girl grow lame,' he'd told the doctors.

They agreed and transferred me to Merlin Park hospital, where Dad demanded a second opinion. His doubts over the amputation were proven right when a senior doctor agreed to operate to save my withered limb. The operation was as gruelling as it was long. The doctor opened up my leg from my knee right down to my ankle to try and kill the infection. It had been such an extensive operation that by the time I eventually regained consciousness, I was bandaged up like an Egyptian mummy. Doctors had initially placed me on an adult ward so that I'd get lots of rest, but instead I was bored out of my brain. With nothing else to do, I decided to teach myself how to read a newspaper. I was nine years old and I was determined not to fall behind the rest of my class.

Astonishingly, the problem with my leg had dragged on for four long years. It hadn't been right since the day I'd stolen the flowers and fallen from the wall into the field. It wasn't until many years later, after the fall, that I discovered what was actually wrong with me. I was diagnosed with something called osteomyelitis – an infection of the bone usually caused by bacteria or fungi. I'd fallen so badly that I'd fractured my leg in the fall and the bone marrow inside had become infected. The condition had blighted my younger years and had left me partially disabled. Stealing the prized daffodils from the doctor's garden had almost cost me my leg and my life.

But if I thought things were bad then, they were about to get a whole lot worse.

# CHAPTER 2

## The Secret

I'd been bedridden after the operation for almost eight months, including a couple of weeks when I'd had to remain completely still and stare at the wall and ceiling. At one point my condition severely worsened and I developed a temperature that left me drifting in and out of consciousness. The doctors eventually managed to get it under control and I started to recover. A month later, I was moved to a children's ward, where I became friendly with a girl in the next bed – her name was Niamh. Although she was my age, Niamh had three holes in her hip and was confined to her bed like me. However, unlike me, Niamh had regular visitors. My family were far too poor to travel the 70 miles, so I was very much alone. I was a nine-year-old child stuck in a sick and withered body, not feeling quite dead or alive but at some stage in between. During my time of convalescence, Niamh and I would listen to a small burgundy transistor radio that her parents had given her to help speed her recovery. She was a kind girl and had asked the nurse to place it in the middle of the ward so that everyone could listen.

'Oh, I love this one!' I shrieked, as 'Walking Back to Happiness' by Helen Shapiro blasted across the hospital ward.

'Me too,' Niamh smiled as we both began to sing along.

The catchy little tune kept me going during the long and boring afternoons spent on the ward. I continued to read because I was eager to learn and not fall behind with my studies. I was so desperate that I'd read religious pamphlets scattered around the ward, anything to keep my brain ticking over.

Niamh's family regularly came from Donegal to visit her, but they must have felt sorry for me because her mother would always bring me fruit.

'Thank you,' I smiled as she handed me a brown paper bag full of juicy grapes.

I was struck by her kindness and by what a loving mother she was – the complete opposite of my own.

The seasons continued to pass with autumn turning into winter, leaving a sprinkling of crisp white snow on the ground outside.

'I wonder what Father Christmas will bring us?' Niamh said, trying to pull herself up in her bed early one morning so that she could peer through the window.

I said nothing. Deep down, I knew I wouldn't get anything for Christmas, not even a visitor. So I was astonished when, a few weeks later and just before Christmas, a nurse came on the ward looking for me. As she approached, I spotted a small brown parcel in her hands.

'This is for you, Mary,' she said, placing it on my bed.

My heart leapt inside my chest with excitement. I wasn't used to presents. Niamh watched and squealed with excitement as I frantically tore open the brown paper to reveal a pair of pink slippers. They'd been sent by Aunt Anne – one of my father's sisters – who lived over in America. I was thrilled because it was the first present I'd received apart from a few from my parents.

'Oh, they're beautiful, Mary!' Niamh gasped as I held them up to look at them.

'Would you like to try them on?' the nurse asked.

I nodded, so she lifted back the cover and placed both slippers on my feet.

'I feel like Cinderella,' I exclaimed as they both began to laugh.

In fact, I felt so special that I didn't stop looking at my feet for the rest of the day. My new and unexpected footwear strengthened my resolve to learn how to walk again. Day by day, I took one, and then two steps. As my wasted muscles began to grow stronger, I took more and more steps. Although I was still shaky on my feet, the doctors decided I was well enough to be discharged. An ambulance was ordered from my hometown of Ballina to come and pick me up and take me home. Sadly, the ambulance driver had other ideas. He'd driven over with Aunt Mary. Unlike Anne, who'd sent the present, Mary had a cruel streak and was determined to get rid of the 'cripple of the family'. Back then, disabled children were considered a curse rather than a blessing, and it wasn't unusual for people to send their kids away to institutions where they could be forgotten and never be seen again. I'd not long boarded the ambulance and had waved goodbye to Niamh and the nurses than we'd taken a detour. Instead of heading straight home as instructed, I was dumped at an old people's home 25 miles away in Castlebar. The home was full of elderly women suffering from dementia – the sort of hellhole you could hide a disabled child. Back then in rural Ireland a lot of county homes took in young children who'd been abandoned or who had 'misbehaved'. Eventually, those same 'forgotten children' were sent to the notorious Magdalene Laundries, where they were left to their own fate. I was still a child, but I'd left one prison only to find myself trapped inside another. I was still weak and sickly but now I had to try and defend myself against women who had not only lost their sanity but their ability to communicate with one another, let alone a young child.

'I'm not meant to be here,' I told a passing nurse, grabbing at her skirt in desperation. I was nine years old and simply terrified.

'Yes, but the driver brought you here, so the doctors must want you to come here for rest.'

I tried to get her to listen, but it was no good. Who'd listen to the pleas of a frightened little girl?

Hours later, I found myself sat at a table alongside the other residents. A door opened and the cook walked into the room carrying a huge tray of baked potatoes. She rested the tray in the middle of the table and, with both hands free, straightened up and wiped her brow with an old dishcloth. I sat and waited, half-expecting someone to come along and serve the potatoes, but instead, a dozen scrawny hands clawed at them, grasping, pulling, and slapping each other to try and pick out the best ones. I blinked and sat wide-eyed as fights proceeded to break out around the table. My nostrils flared with fear, my senses on high alert. The room stank of death. The residents themselves looked like walking skeletons – it was just how I'd imagined hell to be. Once the clawing had finally subsided, I leaned forward and took the last potato from the tray. I was scared, but I was also hungry because I'd eaten nothing since breakfast. Without warning, a hand appeared from nowhere and tried to slap the potato from my grasp. I looked at the old lady sitting next to me.

'Leave alone. That's my food!' she hissed.

She picked up her walking stick and waved it around as though she might beat me.

I flinched and dropped the potato back on the tray. The others stopped what they were doing and looked up as the room fell silent. I'd done nothing wrong but it was clear that the others lived in fear of this woman. I blinked back some tears that had welled up inside my eyes. I desperately wanted to cry because I wanted to be back at home, safe with my family. I tried not to catch the old lady's gaze as my eyes scoured the room for a nurse. But it was empty, apart from me and the table of old ladies.

'Leave her be, Orla. She's just a poor child,' a woman across from me piped up as she began to scold the old woman next to me.

'Stay out of it, Kitty. This is nothing to do with you!'

I glanced across the table at Kitty. She looked as elderly as the others, but she had a kind face.

Orla grunted and pushed her potato into her mouth. She didn't have any teeth so she made a disgusting sound as she licked and sucked at the mush inside her hand. Kitty saw her chance and grabbed the last potato before peeling it and handing it over to me.

'There you go, child,' she said, pressing it into my palm.

I glanced over warily at Orla, who didn't flinch. I was too frightened to say anything – even thank you – so instead I ate in silence with my head bowed. After dinner, the old ladies took to their usual chairs, but I was new and didn't know where to sit. The room had grown cold, so I stood in front of the fire to try and warm myself. I'd only been there a few seconds when I felt a hard shove in the middle of my back. I turned to see Orla standing there, sneering at me.

'Get away from the fire. It's mine!'

I backed away warily. As I did so, I noticed her hand as it hovered over the poker. Her fingers twitched as though they were desperate to grab it and beat me with it. Fear must've shown on my face because Orla began to laugh and soon she couldn't stop herself. She was simply delighted that she'd upset a child. Through her laughter, I heard a voice.

'Come here, child.'

It was Kitty. She was sitting in an old armchair in a corner of the room. She beckoned me over towards her and the safety of her arms and I ran to her as though my life depended on it. For the rest of the week, I lived in constant fear of violent patients, like Orla, who lashed out at me and each other for no reason. Hampered by my limited mobility, I was pushed, bullied, and shoved around the ward; I was a new and easy target to take out their frustrations on. One day, I was sitting in Kitty's arms when she clasped me tight, her claw-like hands holding me still. I was scared but at least I knew I'd be safe there. Although she was old and weak, Kitty had an iron-like grip and her long, yellow fingernails cut against the soft young skin of my arms. I tried to wriggle free but it was impossible. She gripped me until I was anchored there like a baby. I soon realised that in her mind I was.

'There, there, Teresa,' she mumbled softly with her wet mouth against my hair.

As she began to rock me from side to side, a single tear spilled down my cheek. I didn't want Kitty, I wanted my family.

'I want my mammy,' I sobbed as a nurse passed by.

She sighed and came over to prise me from the old lady's arms.

'Get over by your own bed, Kitty. Don't touch the child.'

I was relieved. Relieved that someone was finally on my side. But then the nurse turned to me.

'As for you, keep away from the fire, and keep away from her!' she said, pointing at Orla.

I remained trapped inside that hellhole for almost a week before I was found. When I'd failed to show in Ballina, my father sent word to the hospital in Galway. There was talk of a 'mistake', but I knew it hadn't been, and I was eventually tracked down. Aunt Mary had feigned shock and surprise at the mix-up, but she knew what she'd done. Another ambulance was dispatched and, to my father's relief, I was taken home.

'Come here,' he said, lifting me as though I was made of glass. 'It's so good to have you back home. I've missed you.' Dad ruffled my hair affectionately.

Sadly, my mother didn't seem as happy to see me. As Dad carried me out of the ambulance and inside the house, Mum turned away and said nothing. It was clear that to her I was just another mouth to feed. Although I desperately craved her love, my love for her wasn't reciprocated. I'd been, as the priest had termed it, a 'replacement baby'. My mother had given birth to my older sister, Mary-Jane, who tragically had only lived a few weeks before passing in her sleep. The doctor was unsure what had killed her, but looking back I suspect it must have been cot death. Mum was distraught at losing her second child and only daughter, but as she wept on her knees in front of the priest he'd told her to pull herself together.

'Just go home and make another baby – a replacement baby.'

As callous as it sounds, I'm sure the priest was just trying to shock Mum and pull her from her overwhelming grief. It must have worked, because she did as he said and I was born the following year. However, as the replacement baby I never quite lived up to my dead sister. It was as if, by death alone, Mary-Jane had become a saint. Nothing I could say or do would ever match Mum's high expectations. Instead, I reminded her of the child she'd lost as I continued to disappoint. To make matters worse, she suffered from severe post-natal depression following the birth of each of her children. She'd given birth to six boys and two girls, including baby Bridget. After each, Dad had called for both the priest and doctor, who would admit Mum to the local mental hospital for her own safety. It was a gruelling existence.

When I finally returned home from hospital I couldn't believe how much my baby sister Bridget had grown. She'd gone from being a baby at Mum's breast to a crawling bundle of energy, taking her first steps. Ironically, as she started to walk I remained virtually immobile. Mum doted on Bridget, which made me feel more isolated and unwanted. My mother would store a big pot of water over the fire that she used to wash the children. One day, I was sat in the kitchen, waiting for the water to boil, when she looked over at Bridget, who was playing happily in a corner. My mother's face broke into a huge smile as she watched her infant daughter adoringly.

'Bridget, aren't you beautiful, eh?' she remarked.

Bridget looked up and gave her a big gummy smile that melted my heart. But Mum hadn't finished.

'Bridget,' she called as the baby looked back up. 'Just look at Mary,' she said, gesturing over to me. 'Isn't she ugly? Why, aren't you ugly, Mary?'

Her nasty words hung in the air, but they'd already sliced through the centre of my heart. I wanted to cry, but I didn't want her to know how much she'd hurt me. I loved my baby sister, and I refused to be jealous even when Mum lavished her with love and fancy clothes. It wasn't Bridget's fault she was the favourite daughter, it was Mum's. Bridget was still a baby, she didn't understand. Even though I was young I understood what Mum was doing but I made excuses for her because I also knew she wasn't well. Although I understood, I found it hard to forgive her for the things she said to me then and over the years that followed. When Bridget was two, Mum gave birth to another daughter, who she called Bernadette. I was determined not to be the 'baby' of the family and tried my best to walk and run along with the other children. The doctor had warned my father before the operation that I would be left with one leg shorter than the other.

'But what does that mean? How will it affect her?'

The doctor's response was brutally honest. 'She will be left with a limp and a weakness down that side.'

In spite of the doctor's warning, I vowed to walk as well as my siblings and taught myself to distribute my weight evenly across both legs. This allowed me to walk with a normal gait. I was determined that I wouldn't be known as the 'cripple' of the school. Thankfully, because I had a photographic memory, I was able to catch up at school and push myself forward in class. My mother gave birth to two more children, a boy, and girl, making ten of us in total. Times were tough with a dozen mouths to feed and although Dad was a skilled carpenter, he couldn't always find regular work in Ireland. Instead he'd travel to England, sending his wages back home. After a particularly long stint in England, Dad returned home. By now, I was 12, but I realised from all the rows and raised voices that money was tighter than ever before. There was something else, but I couldn't put my finger on it. I'd often noticed my parents sitting in a corner, talking quietly. As soon as anyone came into the room they'd lower their voices. Something was going on – a secret between them – and it left me feeling uneasy.

One day, my father went to see Anne – his sister who had been living in America. She'd returned home, so the family had gathered at Aunt Nessie's house. I desperately wanted to say thank you for the slippers Anne had sent, so I decided to call on her myself. Balling my hand into a fist, I tapped lightly against the door, stood back, and waited to see who would answer. My father's sisters were all formidable women, who didn't have time for children, everyone apart from Aunt Lily.

'Hello, Mary,' Lily smiled as the door swung open and she found me standing there on the doorstep. 'Well, don't be waiting there letting the cold in, come in, come in.'

I was relieved it had been Lily and not Aunt Nessie. As soon as I entered the house I heard voices deep in conversation. The voices sounded low and serious.

'…but what about Jane and the children?' I heard my father say.

I crept towards the back of the kitchen as quiet as a church mouse and listened. Lily took her place back at the kitchen table as the rest of the sisters advised my father on his best course of action.

'Jane will be fine, and so will the children. They'll have us,' Aunt Nessie insisted, wrapping her hand around Dad's forearm in reassurance. 'Now,' she continued, picking up a huge pot of tea and pouring him another cupful, 'it's the land of opportunity, and you'll never get an opportunity like this again.'

Although I was the eldest girl, back then children were seen and not heard, so I didn't dare interrupt or ask questions. However, even though I was a child I had an uneasy feeling that whatever was being decided at my aunt's table was going to change our lives for ever.

'You should do it, Mickey, you should move to America,' Nessie insisted, slamming the teapot back down on the table. 'We'll look after Jane and the children, won't we?' she said, looking round at the other sisters, who nodded in agreement.

I was scared because I knew my aunts, and all of them, apart from Lily, didn't care for me or my mother. They all loved Dad, but that was where their loyalties began and ended. I slipped silently from Nessie's house and considered what it'd mean. Unlike Mum, my father had always fought my corner. Unlike Mum, he'd listen to me instead of telling me to be quiet. In short, he always had time for me, his eldest surviving daughter. But now everything would be different. My blood ran cold at the thought of having to spend the next few years living alone with Mum. Then something occurred to me – perhaps she didn't know? Taking a huge gulp of air for courage, I ran home to see if there was anything I could do to stop Dad from leaving. As usual, Mum was in the kitchen with a brood of children as I came barging in through the back door.

'What the—? Mary Creighton, don't you be making a mess of my nice clean floor with your filthy boots,' she tutted.

I glanced down, pulled them off, and remained standing there in front of her.

'What?' she asked, straightening up. 'What is it?'

I gulped, balled my hands into small fists for confidence, and then I spoke.

'Is Dad going to America?'

The words just came blurting out. Mum looked shocked, as though I'd slapped her around the face. Then she looked down, unwilling to meet my eye, and I knew then that she knew. That'd been their secret.

'Why? How do you know? Who told you?'

My heart sank to my feet. It was true.

'I heard them... the adults. They were talking about it at Aunt Nessie's house just now. So it's true? Dad is moving to America?'

Mum put down a dirty dishcloth and pulled a stray strand of hair from her face.

'Yes, it's true. Yes, he's going, but we'll all be going soon enough.'

'What? All of us?' I gasped, my voice rising with hope.

Maybe it wasn't such a desperate situation after all. Mum nodded but still refused to look me in the eye. An unsettling feeling nestled in the pit of my stomach and I suddenly felt uncertain and scared for the future. I'd found out what the secret was. My father had often travelled to England for work but he'd only be gone a matter of weeks. America was different because he was going to fly to the other side of the world! Even if it wasn't strictly true, to a child growing up in 1960s rural Ireland it may as well have been. America was so far away. Now the cat was out of the bag it was my secret to keep, and I'd have to hide it from the other children. Mum swore me to secrecy, and I didn't dare slip up and face her temper. Little did I know then, but I wouldn't see my father again until I was a mother myself.

'Go on now, go and see to your sisters and brothers.'

I watched forlornly as the taxi disappeared down the long country road, taking my lovely father away from me. After he'd left Mum insisted I get a job, so after school I started to help a neighbour out with a spot of babysitting and any other chores that needed doing. It only earned me a few bob, but I handed it over to my mother to help feed the little ones. There was no social security then, so everyone was expected to pull their weight. As the eldest girl, that meant doing menial jobs for pennies until Dad sent home his next pay packet. With ten children to care for my mother was vulnerable and so relied on anyone who was willing or able to help. Over the years that followed 'help' arrived in the form of Sister Seraphina, a leading nun in the parish and someone who taught at my school. It's hard to explain, but Sister Seraphina seemed to make our family – and me in particular – her pet project. She'd often look in on other families in the town, but would visit our home every Sunday without fail. Her interest was so intrusive that it felt as though she was spying on us. Looking back as an adult, I'm certain it was more a form of control. Unlike other children at my school, Sister would talk constantly to Mum about me. She'd discuss how much I'd learned in school and what sort of girl I was, and with Dad now gone, it wasn't long before her beady brown eyes were monitoring my every move at home as well. I felt utterly stifled by her. Sister treated me and my siblings as though we were orphans even though we still had both parents. It wasn't long before I grew to resent her interference.

One afternoon there was a knock at the door and I opened it to find Sister Seraphina standing there holding what appeared to be a bundle of rags in her arms.

'Hello, Mary,' she said, without a hint of friendliness. 'Is your mother in?'

'Sister Seraphina,' Mum called out from behind me. 'What a lovely surprise! Well, don't leave Sister standing out there in the cold, Mary. Come in, Sister, come in!'

Sister looked at me as though I was dog muck on the bottom of her shoe as she pushed past me and into the house.

'And to think we teach you manners in school, Mary Creighton,' she tutted loudly. 'You clearly haven't been listening.'

The fact that Sister had scolded me embarrassed my mother, who shot me an icy stare.

I sighed and closed the door behind her because I knew whatever she was here for, it wasn't going to be good. As if I didn't already suffer her enough at school – now here she was almost living at our house. My heart sank as she settled down in her favourite chair – the one by the fire and, incidentally, the best one in the house.

'Mary,' Mum said, snapping me from my thoughts. 'Don't just stand there. Go and fetch Sister a nice cup of tea.'

As the two women began to chat I busied myself boiling a pan of water and set the teapot on the side to warm.

'I hope you don't mind, Jane, but I've brought you some clothes for the children,' Sister said, pointing down at the bundle of rags by her feet.

'No, not at all. You know how difficult things are, what with Mickey working in America.'

Sister Seraphina leaned forward and grabbed my mother's hand in hers. Her face looked concerned, but I knew it was false – she was nothing but an interfering busybody.

'And how are you, Jane? How are you coping?' Sister said, faking concern and trying to dig a little deeper for more information.

I watched from the corner of my eye as Mum sat back and lapped up the attention.

'Well, it's tough, but at least I have my children and my health.'

Sister sat back in her chair, her dark eyes darting over towards me. 'And what about Mary?' she said, as though I wasn't in the room.

'What about her?'

Sister lowered her voice, but the kitchen was small and I could still hear.

'Does she help? She's 13 now, so she should be out working. She's finished school, has she not?'

Mum nodded and Sister Seraphina realised she had her full attention.

'There's nothing worse than a lazy child, Jane,' she whispered conspiratorially. 'You'll end up making a rod for your own back, if you're not careful.'

Mum glanced over and I momentarily caught her eye. I realised I wasn't supposed to be listening so I looked down at the fire and the teapot. The warmth of it reddened my cheeks, masking the anger I felt bubbling up inside.

'She should be working,' Sister continued, tapping her finger against the kitchen table. 'Paying for her keep. Helping her brothers and sisters. Anyway, don't you worry because I've found her the perfect position. She'll be scrubbing floors at St Murdoch's college.'

'St Murdoch's. Really?'

I could tell even with my back turned that Mum was all ears.

Before the tea had even been made it had been decided. I would scrub floors for a Sister Gerard at St Murdoch's college. Sister Gerard ran a very tight ship, according to Sister Seraphina, a comment that made me shudder.

A week or so later, I began my new job. It was a live-in position because the hours were so long, and I was paid 30 shillings a week, which I handed straight to my mother with nothing in return. I worked six and a half days a week, twelve hours a day, from seven in the morning until seven at night. I had to scrub and clean rooms in the college and the private living quarters of the seven priests who taught there. I also had the unenviable task of emptying out their chamber pots. I was young and naive, so when I emptied their chamber pots I thought I was cleaning out phlegm. It was only years later that I realised it was something much nastier indeed. I'd started my new job during the summer holidays, working alongside an older woman called Bridie. She was from County Longford, and had been a cleaner at the college for many years. Bridie was well and truly in the nuns' pockets. Like Sister Gerard, she was a real stickler for getting the best out of her young workers.

'You haven't cleaned between the desks, now, have you?' she said, taking me aside one day. 'Look,' she remarked, pointing down at the floor, 'I can see a stain.'

I shook my head because I knew she was mistaken.

'But they're all done. I've done them all,' I protested.

Bridie's face suddenly changed. I could tell she was annoyed that I'd dared to answer her back.

'No, you haven't! Now you get between those desks now!'

I realised I'd never win, so I did as I was told and pressed in between the desks to clean the floor a second time. The desks were lined up close together inside a grand hall and were heavy, made from mahogany wood. As I squeezed in between the small gap I must have caught my clothes against the side of one because moments later it'd come crashing down on my foot.

SLAM!

'Arrggghhh!'

The noise caused Bridie to turn around sharply. But although the desk was on me and I'd almost fainted with the pain, instead of helping, she seemed angry.

'Well, pick it up then!'

I gasped and looked down as a pool of deep crimson blood began to pool out from inside my shoe. But Bridie had no sympathy and refused to get involved.

'Come on, girl,' she snapped impatiently.

As I lifted up the table my foot slipped out of its shoe and I almost fainted a second time. The impact had severed the main artery in my big toe, which was hanging on by a thread.

'You better go to see Sister Gerard,' Bridie said, recoiling as soon as she saw it. I noticed that her face had suddenly gone ashen.

I slipped my foot halfway back into the shoe because I was worried I'd get into trouble for dripping blood on the floor. Not that it made much difference, because by the time I found Sister Gerard my blood had trailed all along the corridor. Sister was sitting in a linen cupboard, sorting through some bedding, at the top of a flight of stairs when I found her. She looked annoyed as she watched me approach.

'What's the matter, child?' she demanded.

'Sister, it's my foot,' I began. I gestured down to the sore and bloodied mess where my foot was. 'One of the desks fell on it and my toe is hanging off.'

She lifted up her hand, removed her glasses, and shook her head.

'Don't be so ridiculous!'

I didn't move and she realised something serious was wrong. She got to her feet and peered down through the banister railings at me. But her expression changed when she saw the state of my left foot.

'I'll just go and fetch Father Caffery.'

With that she took off down the corridor. Moments later, Father Caffery came rushing over. I think he'd intended to perform some sort of first aid, but as soon as he saw the state of me he thought better of it.

'You need to see the doctor,' he said, reeling back in horror.

Father put me in his car and drove me over to Dr Gallagher's son, who was also a doctor. I just prayed that my run-in with his father over the stolen daffodils had long been forgotten. Once inside, the two men stood over me as Dr Gallagher tried, but failed, to stem the flow of blood.

'I think she needs to go to hospital,' he said, straightening up and finally admitting defeat.

Unfortunately, and for some unknown reason, the only hospital bed available was one on the maternity ward. Sister Gerard must have passed word to my mother, because a few hours later she came flying in through the ward door.

'Where is she? Where's Mary?' I heard Mum's voice call out.

Her eyes scoured the room as a dozen new and expectant mothers looked up. I was so relieved to hear her voice that I called out to her.

'Mammy, I'm in here.'

I waited, relieved that finally I had someone with me in hospital. Moments later a hand pulled back the hospital curtains around my bed. The metal rings scraped against the pole as they parted over to one side. As soon as I saw Mum, I felt better. The nurses had just been dressing my wound and had cleaned it using cotton, water and a bowl, which they'd left at the foot of my bed. Mum's eyes darted from mine to the bloodied bowl and back again. As they did so, her face erupted with anger. She walked over to the side of my bed, lifted her hand, and slapped me hard across my face. The shock of it made me cry out, and I was so stunned that for a moment I couldn't speak. I didn't understand why she had hit me.

'Pregnant! At your age. You disgust me, Mary Creighton!'

I was confused. I wasn't pregnant. Why did she think I was? And then I realised – the bowl of blood and the maternity ward.

'No, no, Mammy, you don't understand,' I said, pulling myself up in my bed.

Her face was crimson with rage as she towered over my hospital bed.

'Oh, I understand all right!'

Her raised voice had alerted a nurse, who came rushing over.

'Mary has hurt her foot,' she began, pointing at the red water inside the bowl. 'We've been trying to stem the flow of blood. It's quite a nasty wound.'

Peeling back the bedcover, she presented my mother with the sight of my badly damaged foot, but Mum remained unconvinced.

'Right, I see,' was all she could say, before she turned and left the hospital.

Doctors eventually managed to stem the blood, but I was told I'd need an operation to stitch my toe back on. A few hours later I was transferred to Castlebar hospital, where they tried to save my foot. A doctor had warned me that I'd never wear a shoe again because the accident had damaged my toenail, leaving it vertical rather than horizontal. The desk had crushed the bone in my toe so badly that it'd crumbled and it looked as though I only had three-quarters of a toe. I underwent an operation later the same day, and remained in hospital for over a month. Eventually, I was discharged and brought back home by ambulance. As it pulled up outside the house, Mum was waiting for me.

'And don't be thinking you can sit there all day doing nothing,' she said as soon as I'd hobbled back in. 'I've got enough to do without having to run around after the likes of you.'

Once I was finally up and about on my feet again, Mum insisted that I go back to the college to ask for my old job back. However, Sister Gerard had other ideas.

'The job is no longer available,' she replied curtly.

Sister had realised I had a strong case against the college for compensation so she intended to get rid of me as soon as possible.

'And close the door on your way out,' she added as I turned to leave.

As for Mum, she never apologised for wrongly assuming I'd been pregnant. In fact, from that moment on, she blamed me not only for the accident, but for losing my job.

# CHAPTER 4

## The Pregnancy

After losing my job at the college I was desperate to find other employment to keep my mother off my back, if nothing else. We'd never been close, but with Dad now gone, she found it hard to hide her resentment towards me. I seemed to be a constant disappointment. Thankfully, I managed to secure a job working in a rubber factory making wellington boots and buckets. My job was mind-numbingly boring; trimming the edge off wellies and packing them into boxes, but it brought in a wage so it kept Mum happy. I worked hard over the next few months and soon I'd come to the attention of old Mrs Neil, the factory owner.

'Mary, how old would you be?' she said, leaning up against my workbench on the factory floor one afternoon.

'Fourteen, miss.'

'Is that all?' she exclaimed. 'Well, I think this work is far too heavy for a young girl like you.'

It didn't feel particularly heavy, but I didn't argue with her because she was the boss. At the same time, I didn't want to lose another job.

'Listen,' Mrs Neil said, looking down at me. 'My daughter is a busy lady and she needs help with her boys and housework. I think that type of work might be a little more suited to a girl like you, don't you think?'

Even though I was still a teenager, I realised it was more a request than a question. Mrs Neil's daughter needed a young girl to babysit and the old lady had decided I would do it, even though it would be a live-in position.

'Yes,' I replied, without realising what I'd let myself in for.

Mrs Neil's daughter, Gael Lafferty, was in her early thirties and was mother to three young boys. There was seven-year-old William, Kevin, who was four, and John, the baby of the family at just 18 months old. As the eldest girl, I'd often looked after my sisters and brothers, so both Mrs Lafferty and her mother were confident that I had more than enough experience for the position. On my first day, I approached the gates of the house. Although I could see the black wrought-iron gates and two empty fields either side, I couldn't see the house. I pushed open the gate and let myself in, but there was still no sign of the house. There was a forest in front of me so I walked through it until I reached a clearing, and that's when I saw it – the Laffertys lived in a mansion, not a house. To a working-class girl it seemed like a palace, both inside and out. In fact, it only had four bedrooms. However, the size of the hallway and other rooms more than made up for its lack of bedrooms. I hesitated slightly as I lifted my hand and knocked at the door. It seemed to take an age for someone to answer, and when someone finally did, I was surprised when it turned out to be Mrs Lafferty herself.

'Oh, you must be Mary,' she said, smiling down at me warmly.

Tall, and with long dark hair and breathtaking beauty, Mrs Lafferty held out her long and slender white hand, shook mine, and welcomed me inside. As I looked up at the oil paintings on the wall and the grand china resting on the side, it became evident that the family had money. This made it all the more surprising that the lady of the house had answered her own front door. Where is the staff? I wondered.

'The children are through here, if you'd like to meet them,' Mrs Lafferty said, leading me into a side room.

I followed her through to a large room, where the three boys were playing on the floor with wooden toys. As soon as we entered the room they looked up at me quizzically.

'This is Mary,' Mrs Lafferty said, directing her words at William, the eldest boy. 'She's come to look after you.'

I smiled at them half-heartedly. Even though I'd looked after my own siblings, standing there inside the big posh house I felt completely out of my depth. I was terrified of doing something wrong and losing my new job. I wasn't sure what to do, so I got down on my hands and knees and began playing with the boys so that they'd feel comfortable with me. Afterwards, I cooked us all some lunch. A few hours later, Mrs Lafferty came into the kitchen, looking for me.

'I thought you might like these,' she said, handing over a pair of beautiful royal blue trousers and a pale blue top.

'Thank you,' I gasped. I was overwhelmed because I'd only just met her and I wasn't used to such gifts or kindness.

Although she was generous, it wasn't long before I realised that gifts came at a price. It soon became apparent that Mrs Lafferty was a social butterfly, who liked to host grand dinner parties in her large and imposing home. Being a perfectionist, everything had to be just so and exactly as she liked it. Although I never saw or met any of her guests, the following morning I knew they'd been there because it was left to me to clean up their mess. Mrs Lafferty and her husband Liam travelled to Dublin every weekend. Mr Lafferty was a commercial traveller, trading mainly in high-end fashion clothing and millinery. The couple had owned a slipper factory in England, but it had closed down, so they'd returned to Ireland to help run the family business. I soon discovered that they employed a team of six girls, who worked Monday to Friday, from 8am to 5pm. The girls would sew scarves in one of the downstairs rooms. I'd often heard chatter and the whir of sewing machines from behind closed doors, but I never met or even saw them because I was too busy looking after the Lafferty children. Although it was a live-in position, I wasn't just a nanny; I also cooked family meals, laundered clothes, and cleaned the house to Mrs Lafferty's exacting standards. Back then, there was no such thing as a washing machine so all the clothes had to be washed by hand. It was thoroughly exhausting work, even for a teenage girl. The reality of my new job became clear: I was paid to look after the children, but for all the other work I was doing I was an unpaid skivvy. In spite of this, I couldn't help but like Mrs Lafferty.

Mr Lafferty, on the other hand, was an entirely different matter. I was only 14 and still going through puberty, but he would always find a reason to be alone in a room with me. He'd 'accidentally' brush up against me whenever we were in an enclosed space, usually when I was standing in front of the sink washing the dishes. If that wasn't bad enough, he'd always turn the conversation around to something sexual. Even though he was in his mid-forties, he regularly made inappropriate remarks about my body that left me feeling on edge.

'Tell me, Mary,' he began one day, leering over at me from the kitchen table. I felt my heart sink as he got to his feet and pushed up against me in an attempt to look down my top. 'How old are you again?'

My nostrils flared and my senses were on high alert because he was close – *too* close. Now that he was, I could smell the Irish whiskey and cigarettes on his breath that was hot against my skin.

'14. I'm, erm, 14, sir,' I said, trying to focus on the dinner plate in my hand. I scrubbed at an imaginary mark on the porcelain. Anything had to be better than having to look at him.

'Fourteen, you say?' he leered, showing off his yellow, nicotine-stained teeth.

He pushed the whole of his body against me as he brushed past and leaned against the work surface next to me. I could sense him standing there, staring at me, and undressing me with his eyes. The silence between us was excruciating, so I spoke to ease the tension.

'Yes, sir. That's right, I'm 14.'

I remained focused on the plate in my hands. I didn't look up because I didn't want to see his smarmy face.

'Well,' he said, pulling a silver cigarette holder from his pocket. He held it in one hand, flipped it open, and withdrew a cigarette. Sulphur rose up into my nostrils as he struck a match, and then a bluish grey cloud of smoke curled its way through the air as he blew it out from the side of his mouth. 'You're certainly developing, aren't you?' he whispered against my ear.

I felt my flesh crawl.

'I beg your pardon?'

'Pardon?' he laughed, mocking me. I felt my cheeks burn hot with embarrassment.

Every sinew in my body told me to run as fast and as far away from him as possible, but he was the boss – the master of the house – and I was his employee. I also had to finish the dishes. If I didn't then Mrs Lafferty would want to know why, and I could hardly tell her about her husband or his wandering hands. Instead, I concentrated on the sink and told myself to try and not react, but it was too late. He'd already seen me blush and he knew he'd got to me. It was a game of cat and mouse, with him the cat and me the mouse. From that moment on I vowed to avoid him.

I'd been at the house for around a month when Mrs Lafferty hosted another one of her legendary dinner parties. I'd gone up to my room when the party was in full swing, but I'd awoken halfway through the night with a terrible thirst. Pulling on my dressing gown, I nipped downstairs to get myself a glass of water. I was just filling a glass at the kitchen sink when I heard an almighty scream and almost dropped the glass in fright. I dashed out into the hallway to see Mrs Lafferty running down the grand staircase. Her candlewick dressing gown gaped open, revealing her stark naked body. I'd heard raised voices earlier that evening, but the Laffertys would often argue so I'd thought no more of it. But now Mrs Lafferty seemed frightened and headed straight for the telephone to call for help. I went over to her, but as soon as she spotted me she blushed as though ashamed. Self-consciously pulling her dressing gown tight around her body, she wiped her tear-stained eyes with one sleeve and returned to her bedroom without another word.

I wasn't quite sure what to do. For a moment I remained standing there, wondering if I should follow. I was worried Mr Lafferty might have hurt her in some way. But then I heard the click of their bedroom door as she closed it behind her. I grabbed my glass and went back to bed, but I couldn't sleep because I was too busy listening out for her.

As the weeks passed by, the rows increased in their frequency, but I soon realised it was him and not her. Mr Lafferty was unpredictable, with a hair-trigger temper, because he was an alcoholic. His daily sexual harassment of me continued, but I never told a soul because I didn't want to add to his wife's ongoing marital problems.

A short while later, I was cleaning their bedroom and changing the sheets on their bed when I came across a cream-coloured balloon. I was a shy Catholic girl, so that's what I assumed it was. Thinking the boys would be delighted, I took the balloon downstairs, filled it with water, and gave it to William to play with. I spotted Mrs Lafferty in an upstairs window, watching as the children played with it in the garden all afternoon. She obviously knew what it was but chose not to say. Every time I cleaned the bedroom I'd find another balloon. Soon, curiosity had got the better of me and I found myself looking to see where they had come from and why they were always on the floor at the side of the bed. Pulling open a cupboard in Mrs Lafferty's dressing table, I spotted a large box – a box full of condoms. Back then in Ireland, condoms were unheard of because Catholics weren't meant to use birth control. But it seemed Mrs Lafferty had had enough of her lecherous husband and his constant demands for sex that she chose to protect herself, religion or no religion. Sadly, my own naivety soon caught up with me.

One rare night off, I decided to walk into town because there was a horror film I wanted to see on at the pictures. After it'd finished I started to walk the three miles back home when I got talking to a tall and handsome boy called Mickey. Unlike other boys, Mickey made me laugh and seemed so much more mature than other lads I'd met. He was charming and full of compliments, which made me feel special and loved. Although he came from a working-class background like me, he was kind and treated me like a lady. Nothing was ever too much trouble, and that made me feel very special indeed. It was something I'd never experienced with a boy before, and soon I'd come to trust him. Before long, we started going out together and would arrange to meet up on the road to Ballina. Mickey was a few years older than me and much more experienced in all things sexual. A simple kiss soon turned into fondling, and eventually sex, not that I realised or even knew that's what it was – I didn't even know where babies came from.

One weekend the Laffertys were over in Dublin as usual, so Mickey persuaded me to invite him back to the house.

'I'd love to see it, Mary. To see the inside of it.'

I hesitated because I knew I wasn't allowed to have guests. But Mickey wore me down, so I relented and told him to call round once they'd left. When I spotted him walking towards the house I waved him in through the back door and up into my room. I'd already put the three boys to bed, but William woke up a few hours later to go to the bathroom, passing by my bedroom as he did so.

'Who's that?' he asked, standing sleepy-eyed in the doorway.

His voice had startled me because I wasn't expecting him to be up at that time.

'Never you mind,' I said, closing the door on Mickey in the bedroom behind. 'Now let's get you to the toilet and then straight back to bed.'

I vowed never to bring my boyfriend to the house again.

'I'll get into trouble, I'll lose my job,' I fretted.

But Mickey seemed more relaxed.

'He's only a kid, he won't say anything. He'll think he was dreaming.'

But he was wrong. The following morning, William told his mother that I'd had a boy in my room. Mrs Lafferty didn't say a word; instead, she let me take the children to school as normal. It wasn't until I returned that she confronted me. As soon as I approached the house, she flung the door wide open. 'You've had a fella in here, haven't you?' she hollered across the driveway.

My heart leapt inside my chest because I knew I'd been rumbled. With a dry mouth, my mind scrambled for the right words as I tried to think what to say. I knew there wasn't any point in lying because lies always end up catching you out. Instead, as I walked inside the house I decided to tell the truth.

'Yes, but I didn't do anything with him.'

'But you had him in your bedroom,' she insisted, her eyes boring into me with every single word.

I looked up at her, hoping for forgiveness.

'We didn't do anything, I promise. We were just talking.'

But Mrs Lafferty was horribly disappointed in me, and that made me feel worse. Grabbing the top of a chair with her hand, she pointed over towards the door.

'You're sacked. Get out of my house now!'

Tears pricked at the back of my eyes, but I did as I was told. There was no point in trying to argue. Instead, I went to my room, packed a bag, and left the Laffertys' house for good. With nowhere else to go I found myself walking back into my mother's kitchen. She was busy tending to my younger brother and sister, but as soon as she heard me come in she turned sharply on her heels.

'Why are you here? What's happened? You better not have lost your job, Mary Creighton,' she said, wagging a finger.

'It's Mrs Lafferty,' I began. 'She says she needs someone older to look after the children. I'm not needed any more.'

It was a lie, and I didn't usually tell lies, but the thought of my mother discovering the real reason had seemed much more daunting. She had no connection to the Laffertys, so I knew she'd never discover the real reason for my sudden unemployment. Despite him costing me my job, I still loved Mickey, and our relationship continued. Soon we'd been going out almost eight months. Mickey's sister owned a flat in town, and he decided to take full advantage of both it and me. I was only 15, but my clothes suddenly began to feel a lot tighter. One summer's morning, my mother sent me on an errand to buy milk, Brasso, and bleach.

'Don't be dilly-dallying now, I need you home to help me with the children.'

I picked up the goods and made my way back home. I put the milk and bleach on the table and walked through to the other room with the Brasso still in my hand. As I leaned forward to pick something up I felt a warm sensation against my chest. I glanced down, and to my horror, I realised that both my breasts were leaking. My stomach flipped with fear. I lifted a hand and pressed it against one breast, but I almost fainted when milk came flooding out. I wandered outside and gulped down some fresh air. I was still in shock when I bumped into Mrs Fleming, a friend and neighbour.

'Hello, Mary, how are you?' she said, smiling breezily as she approached.

My face must have given me away because she immediately put her hand on my arm and asked if I was all right.

I nodded, but I could tell she wasn't convinced.

'Are you sure?' She eyed me with suspicion. 'It's just that you've been going mad for those ice lollies lately.'

I trusted Mrs Fleming, and I was worried about the stains on my dress and what it meant. There was nothing else for it, I had to tell her. As soon as I did her face dropped.

'Mary,' she gasped. 'You're having a baby. You have to tell your mother.'

I started to shake until soon my whole body was quivering with fear. Mum would kill me!

'B... but I don't know how to...' I stammered.

I needed time to think, but I was too scared to return home so instead I went looking for Mickey. His face broke into a huge smile as I walked towards him, but then he spotted my tear-stained face and came running over.

'Mary,' he said, his eyes searching mine, 'whatever's the matter?'

I swallowed down my nerves, looked at him, and spoke.

'Mickey, I think I'm having a baby,' I said, blurting the words out too quickly.

Tears began to flow down my cheeks as shock registered on his face. He stood there open-mouthed as I waited for him to say something, anything.

There was a moment's silence and then he spoke. 'I'll marry you, Mary.'

My heart lifted. Maybe this would be all right? After all, Mickey loved me and I loved him. We would and could get through this together. I was just planning our future together when I remembered something.

'How on earth am I going to tell my mother?'

Mickey straightened himself up.

'I'll tell her. I'll come with you now.'

I was dreading telling her the news, but I also knew I couldn't keep it a secret any longer. I was pregnant with Mickey's baby, but he was a decent lad and he'd just said he wanted to marry me. Everything will be all right, I told myself. I'd become a mother and Mickey's wife all in one go, even though I was still only 15.

We walked back to Mum's house in virtual silence. On the way, Mickey grabbed hold of my hand, which made me feel better, stronger somehow. As soon as we walked into the kitchen, Mum knew something was up. She was sat in a chair by the range, but she looked up expectantly, waiting for one of us to speak.

'Mrs Creighton,' Mickey began, nervously clearing his throat. 'I want to marry your daughter. I want to marry Mary.'

Mum had some knitting needles in her hands, but as soon as he spoke she put them down. Her eyes darted between Mickey's and mine.

'Is there a reason?'

He looked her square in the eye. 'She's having my baby.'

Mum's expression changed as though the blood had drained from her. I'd expected shouting and name-calling, but for once she was quiet.

'Well, we'll see about this,' she said, returning to her knitting.

The needles clicked and clacked in her hands as she ignored us and focused on the job in hand. We weren't sure what to do so we both went outside for some fresh air. Standing outside the back door, Mickey grabbed my hand again.

'I *will* marry you.'

'I know.' I smiled. I didn't doubt him for a minute.

The following day, Mum continued her silence so Mickey and I walked over to the priest's private residence to speak with him.

'It's Mary,' Mickey began, gesturing over towards me. 'I'd like to marry her as soon as possible.'

The priest looked up and nodded his head. His eyes lingered on my dress, which strained against my pregnant body. It was clear why there was such urgency.

'I can marry you but you'll need both parents' consent to it taking place because you are so young.'

My heart sank because I realised what that meant.

'But my father's in America. I don't even know how to get in touch with him.'

But the priest was both unmoved and unconcerned.

'I'm sorry, but you'll need both his and your mother's permission if you want to go ahead.'

With no parental consent we realised there could be no marriage. Instead, I returned to my mother and her silent fury. Mum and I didn't speak very much after that, only when housework and chores needed to be done. But time was running out and something needed to be done and fast. A week later, Sister Seraphina turned up unannounced on our doorstep. I'd not seen her in a while because I'd been working away from home at the Laffertys. But now she'd reappeared like a proverbial bad penny.

'Come in, Sister,' Mum said as though she'd been expecting her.

She showed her into the kitchen, leaving me in the other room as they went through to discuss something in private. Moments later, I heard Sister's voice calling me in. I went into the kitchen, where they were both sat at the table, staring at me.

'Now, Mary, you'll be going away to have this baby,' Sister said as soon as I'd entered the room. She placed both hands flat against the top of both knees as if to confirm her words. 'You'll go to a mother-and-baby home in Castlepollard. It is where you'll have the baby, which will then be adopted.'

I gasped in horror. 'What do you mean, adopted?'

Just saying the word made me feel sick.

'You will not be keeping that baby, Mary,' Sister insisted. 'You are going to Castlepollard, where you will be having that baby, and you don't tell anyone about it. It's best all round because no one will want you.'

I glanced over her shoulder at Mum, my eyes scouring her face, pleading for her to fight my corner. But she showed no emotion. Instead, she seemed defiant, as though the decision had already been made. I backed away from them like a trapped animal and wrapped both hands around my growing baby bump. It was autumn 1967. I'd recently celebrated my 16th birthday, so I was still a youngster myself, but I knew that I had to protect my unborn child – to protect it from them and their wicked plans. But neither of them seemed interested in what I wanted or had to say.

'I want to keep it,' I said as tears flowed down my face. Soon, my body was racked with pitiful sobs.

'Mickey wants to marry me,' I wept. 'We're going to be a family. I'll be able to have the baby and—'

But Mum had heard enough. She held up a hand to shush me as her dark eyes darted between Sister Seraphina and me.

'Look, Mary, this is the best thing for it.'

'But—'

'Enough!' she snapped. 'I feel like putting you up them stairs, putting the bed leg on your stomach, and sitting on it to get rid of that thing!'

I looked at her aghast. This was my baby but she was talking about it as though it was a small inconvenience – a problem that needed to be dealt with. I realised then I was all alone. It'd been a week since I'd seen Mickey – something that spoke volumes. His initial desire to do the right thing and marry me seemed to have evaporated, and now I was on my own and at the mercy of Sister and my mother. Mickey had abandoned me, just like everyone else. The decision had already been made, Sister insisted, as I sat crying in the corner.

'Come to your old school tomorrow morning. Be there at half past eight, and don't be late!'

'Don't worry, Sister, she won't be,' Mum butted in, answering for me.

I knew then from that moment on my life would no longer be my own.

# CHAPTER 5

## The Mother-
## and-Baby Home

I was five months pregnant when I walked towards my old school and to what was to become my new life. It was Friday, 4th October. I really didn't want to leave Ballina, but now that Mickey seemed to have disappeared off the face of the earth I realised I had very little choice. My mother waved me off with a brood of children hanging off her apron at the back door, but there were no hugs and no kisses from her, just a curt 'goodbye'.

Pushing open the door to the school, I immediately heard Sister's voice calling out my name. Although I was bang on time, she was already there waiting for me.

'Come in, Mary, and close the door behind you,' she whispered as though this was a secret best kept between us.

I turned, closed the door, and walked over towards her.

'Now,' she said, glancing down at my smart blouse, reefer jacket, and grey tartan skirt, 'you need to come to the toilet with me.'

I wasn't sure why she wanted me to go to the toilet, but I knew better than to disobey. I reluctantly followed her, but as we passed the girls' toilets she kept on walking and I wondered where on earth she was taking me. We continued along the school corridor and down towards the nuns' toilet – a place I'd never been before. Suddenly, I felt extremely awkward and I hesitated in the doorway like a naughty child.

'Come on,' Sister said, beckoning me in. 'Don't worry yourself now, Mary, because it's all going to be fine. Come in and take your clothes off.'

Sister was a tall, odd-looking woman – a dead ringer for the actor Kenneth Williams. To say she gave me the creeps would have been an understatement.

'What do you want me to take my clothes off for?' I asked warily.

'I've got these clothes for you,' she said, producing a bundle from inside a cupboard at the side of the room. 'You'll not be needing those clothes any longer – they'll be no good to you now.'

Sister was standing there with both arms extended as she took my jacket and skirt. Her eyes never once left me, which made me feel extremely uncomfortable.

'Come on, I need your blouse as well,' she said, waving her fingers to hurry me up.

I shuddered. My flesh crawled underneath her steely gaze. I hated being there with her – a nasty old woman, who was making me strip inside a freezing cold toilet. I wanted to refuse, but she'd insisted that she was going to help and I had no other option. For now I'd have to trust her and do as she said. Her eyes were still on me as I stripped down to my vest and knickers. I was young, uncertain, and insecure about my growing, pregnant body. She gathered my clothes into a bundle in her hands and pushed them inside a bag. Then she handed me a washed-out black skirt that went down to my ankles – exactly the type an old lady would wear. I glanced forlornly at the bag on the floor. It contained my old clothes and my old life – one that didn't exist any more. Inside I felt a part of me die.

'Here's something to put on your top half,' she said, handing me a baggy T-shirt. It swamped my small frame but conveniently hid my baby bump below a mound of ugly grey cotton.

I discovered the black skirt had plastic runners stitched onto the sides of it because I could feel them digging against my skin. At first I wondered what they were, and then I realised: they were there to allow the skirt to grow with my baby. I looked down and hardly recognised myself: I was wearing a stranger's clothes and soon I'd be shipped to a strange place. I wondered who the clothes had once belonged to and what had happened to their previous owner. Maybe they'd once belonged to a girl like me who had found herself in trouble? Maybe her future, like mine, had fallen into the hands of Sister Seraphina and the Catholic Church? As I gazed down at the clothes I wondered what would become of me. Maybe all those clothes she'd brought to our house over the years had been taken from other families. Maybe their children had been passed around like worthless rags as I was now. My thoughts were broken by Sister's voice, which sounded cold and business-like.

'A social worker, Mrs Elroy, will be joining us on the journey to Castlepollard. Come on, now, hurry up!'

I laced up my shoes and dragged my hands through my long mousey brown hair. I needed to comfort myself with something familiar because I no longer looked or felt like myself any more. Sister left the room and told me to follow. We walked along the corridor, with me walking a few steps behind, until we'd reached the main entrance. She sat down by the door and gestured for me to do the same but I remained standing.

'Wait there. Mrs Elroy will be here soon.'

I didn't know Mrs Elroy, or this strange place called Castlepollard, where nuns sent you to give birth and have your baby taken from you. Everything felt odd and out of place.

'But what if I don't want to go? What if I want to stay here and keep my baby?'

Sister turned in her seat and fixed her eyes on me. Her eyes were so dark that they looked like the pit of hell. Her voice showed no trace of emotion as she spoke. Instead, her words were as sharp as a jagged piece of glass, and as cutting.

'Well, you should have thought of that before you gave yourself to that boy, shouldn't you?' she said, spitting the words out. 'As it stands, you don't have much choice. In fact, you should be grateful that your mother asked me to help, otherwise heavens knows where you'd be.'

I averted my eyes towards the ground. I felt small and ashamed. I'd just turned 16, and I was supposed to have my whole life ahead of me, but now it felt as though it was over before it'd even begun. My pregnancy had brought shame on myself and my family, and now I'd pay for my mistake. I went over to a chair near the entrance and sat down beside her. I thought about Mickey. Did he know I was being sent away? Did he even care?

I glanced up at the door and pictured him bursting through to rescue me. But deep down, I knew that only happened in fairy tales. This was real life, and, as the minutes ticked by, I knew he'd never come. I was in the hands of Sister, and only God could help me now.

Suddenly I heard the sound of a car engine as a vehicle approached and then stopped on the road outside. My ears strained, listening for more clues. This was it: it was time.

'Come on now, Mary. She's here, and you don't want to keep her waiting.'

Sister rose to her feet and opened up the door. The cold, fresh morning air hit my skin as autumn sunlight came flooding into the vestibule. Blinking against the morning light, my new stranger's clothes felt thin and inadequate against the cool breeze. I shivered. I wasn't sure if it was with cold or fear of what awaited me and my unborn child at the other end. I glanced towards the road. A cream-coloured ambulance had parked up in the road outside. An unfamiliar man got out of the driver's seat. He didn't say a word or even look at me as he opened up the back door and I climbed in. The social worker was sitting there waiting. A small woman, with severe brown hair, sprinkled with strands of silver, Mrs Elroy directed me to the seat next to her, patting a hand impatiently against it as she did so.

'You're going to a mother-and-baby unit at Castlepollard,' she explained. 'Now, I want no nonsense from you, understand? You'll hear from me again in due course when the baby's born. I'll be back when he or she is six weeks old.'

I nodded to show that I understood. By the tone of her voice I could tell that she'd already judged me. I knew she had me down as some backward country girl. She'd just spoken to me as though I was illiterate, when in reality, I could read and write better than anyone I knew. Not that that would help me now. Sister Seraphina climbed in, the door slammed shut, and we set off. We travelled in silence as the ambulance drove down one country lane after another. The journey seemed to go on forever and each minute dragged as the countryside whizzed by in a blur. I peered through the brown-tinged ambulance window, safe in the knowledge that I could look out but others couldn't see in. It brought me small comfort – I felt hidden with my 'shame' from the rest of the world. I gently clasped a hand around my stomach to try and feel the life within. I cringed as I thought of Dad and what he'd say. I imagined his disappointment and it made me sad. Specks of rain pattered softly against the windows, mirroring how miserable I felt inside. There was a swishing noise as the driver turned on the windscreen wipers as the rain grew heavier. I wondered if he judged me as much as the two women. It seemed that everyone thought I was no good, and right now, I felt it.

An hour or so into the journey, Sister leaned forward towards me, trying to strike up a conversation.

'This is for the best now, Mary. You need to put everything else out of your head.' She patted my knee lightly as though I was a dog who needed to learn how to behave.

I looked at her but I didn't reply because there were no words for how I was feeling. Her head swayed from side to side as the road bumped along beneath us. I was certain she was trying to brainwash me, to make me understand that I had no choice. She wanted me to know that right now, here inside this ambulance, my life was no longer my own.

Eventually, we came to a halt. I heard the driver's door click open and slam shut as he climbed out and opened up the back doors. Light streamed inside, momentarily blinding me. As my eyes adjusted I noticed that we'd pulled up outside a large bleak building surrounded by countryside. The driver held out his hand and I stepped down on to the path. Sister, Mrs Elroy and I approached the main entrance of the three-storey building, where a nun was already waiting to greet me. The three women exchanged pleasantries and we made our way into a large sitting room, where the nun told me to take a seat. Meanwhile, the women converged in a far corner of the room to discuss me in low voices.

'Thank you,' the younger nun eventually said, signalling that the meeting was over. She said farewell to the women and led them back into the corridor. 'I will take the child from here.'

I looked over to see Sister Seraphina and Mrs Elroy disappear without a second glance. I pictured them as they climbed into the back of the ambulance – the last link to my former life – and drove away, leaving me to my fate.

The young nun who greeted me stepped back into the room. She was extremely thin, and totally unlike the older nuns I'd met before. I had hoped that her youth would make her kinder perhaps, but I was wrong.

'My name is Sister Justina,' she said.

'I'm Mary,' I replied. My voice sounded different – reedy and thin.

'Francesca,' she corrected before walking back towards the door.

I turned my head and looked behind me. I'd half-expected another girl to be standing behind, but we were all alone in the room.

'I'm speaking to you,' Sister said, turning impatiently.

'But that's not my name. My name is Mary,' I repeated, thinking she'd misheard me. 'I think you've got the wrong girl.'

'No, it is Francesca for as long as you are under this roof. You are Francesca. Now, come on. Don't be standing there. Follow me. You need to get to work.'

I was confused but did as she said. As we walked along the corridor we were joined by two other girls. Both were heavily pregnant, but neither of them said a word to me or each other. Instead, we robotically followed Sister. I didn't understand why I had to change my name, but I was too scared to ask. Suddenly we came to a halt. She opened a door and pointed at the room inside.

'Wait here. Someone will be with you shortly.'

She closed the door and I turned to scan the room. There wasn't much inside it other than a large table and a line of wooden chairs. I wasn't sure whether I should sit or stand. My legs ached, even though I'd been sat inside the ambulance. The sudden effects of my pregnancy had become all too real. Moments later, the door opened and the two girls walked in. The older girl was carrying a huge mound of cotton wool that she placed in a cloud-like mound on the table in front of me.

'You need to make cotton wool balls with this,' she instructed.

My mouth gaped open, and a brief moment passed with me staring at the girls and the table full of cotton wool.

'Didn't you hear me? I said you have to sit here and make cotton wool balls,' she repeated.

I shook my head.

'I'm not touching it,' I decided, resting back in my chair with both arms folded across my chest.

The girl looked over at me a little exasperated, but her voice was kind.

'You have to, otherwise you'll get into trouble.'

I was thoroughly exhausted from the long journey, and the thought of handling squeaky dry cotton wool had set my teeth of edge. But I'd only just arrived at Castlepollard and I didn't want to make enemies. I thought for a moment, picked up a handful of cotton, and began rolling it between my palms.

'That's it,' the older girl said, sitting down, trying to encourage me.

I smiled. It wasn't her fault. They were obviously in the same boat as me – both were unmarried mothers. For once it felt good to be the same as everyone else and not an outsider.

'How many do I have to make?'

The girl looked up and nodded at the huge mound of cotton wool on the table between us.

'Until all that is gone.'

I gasped.

'But there's so much of it!'

She shrugged.

'Doesn't matter. If you don't finish it then you'll get into trouble with the nuns, and you don't want to do that.'

'But what is it for? The cotton wool?'

The older girl looked at me as though it should be obvious. She placed a hand against her heavily swollen stomach.

'The babies, of course. The nuns take it and put it through a sterilising machine.'

Then she stood up, went out of the door, and pulled a large empty metal container into the room, parking it up at the side of the table.

'When they're done, put them in there,' she said, pointing down at it.

I gasped in astonishment. The container was absolutely huge.

'What? You mean I have to fill it?'

'Yes. You have to use all the cotton wool and you can't stop until you have.'

Soon my hands felt itchy, dry, and stiff from making thousands of tiny balls. The joints of my fingers ached where I'd been pulling and rolling it. It had seemed an impossible task in the beginning but slowly the container began to fill up with white clouds of cotton wool. The girls had left me to it, but a couple of hours later, two others appeared.

'Would you like a cup of tea?' a girl with red hair asked, popping her head around the door.

I nodded gratefully. My throat felt scratchy from breathing in the cotton fibres. I drank the cup of tea greedily as they both looked on. The older girl had dark hair and was in her twenties. She looked more pregnant than the red-haired girl. In fact, she looked as though she was about to give birth any day. The red-haired girl, who looked about 18, had seemed less pregnant but she was still further on than me at around six months.

'You need to work fast,' the younger one remarked. 'Sister Justina will come back to see if you're doing a good job.'

Although my fingers were aching I did as she said and speeded up my pace.

'So,' I said, trying to make conversation with the older one. 'When's your baby due?'

She cradled her hands against her stomach.

'Oh, not long now. How about you?'

'I'm not sure,' I answered truthfully. 'I didn't even realise I was pregnant until recently.'

Both girls glanced at each other and then over at me in pity.

'How old are you?' the younger one asked.

'I've just turned 16.'

They tried to hide it but I could tell they were shocked. It was clear I was young to be a mother, even in a place like this. The more we chatted, the more I realised the girls were exactly the same as me. I blushed as I recalled how rude I must have seemed to the first two girls, refusing to do the work as though I was somehow better.

'So, what are your names?'

'This is Bree,' the older one replied, 'and my name is Siobhan.'

'Are they your real names?'

They both shook their heads. It transpired that no one was allowed to use her real name at Castlepollard.

'No, they're our house names,' Siobhan replied. 'Why, what's your name?'

I sighed and put down the cotton wool for a moment.

'Well, Sister told me I'm called Francesca, even though my name is Mary. I wouldn't mind, but I don't even like Francesca.'

Siobhan and Bree burst out laughing as I rolled my eyes in mock annoyance. I knew then we would all get on famously.

Just then, the door creaked open and Sister Justina popped her head around it.

'Ah, I see you're doing a very good job there, Francesca. Very nice.'

Then she disappeared.

I chatted with the two girls long into the afternoon. They both sat down and began to help me clear the mound of cotton from the table, their fingers working twice as quickly as mine. Before I knew it, we'd made thousands of cotton wool balls and had almost filled the container to the brim. By the time I'd gathered the last fibres of cotton the sky had turned dark outside.

'What time is it?' I asked Siobhan.

'I have no idea. They don't have any clocks at Castlepollard, but it's dark so it must be dinner time.'

'Good,' I said, rubbing my stomach, 'because I'm starving. I haven't eaten all day.'

With the work done, I followed the girls into a huge hall, where there were dozens of young women in various states of pregnancy. There were all ages, although it soon became apparent that I was the youngest one there. Siobhan and Bree wandered off to sit at another table, and suddenly I felt a little lost. There were four seats to each table but I wasn't sure where I should sit or if there was any order to it.

'Here,' a girl called over to me. She gestured to an empty chair right next to her. 'You can come and sit here, if you like?'

I smiled gratefully and sat down beside her.

'What's your name?' she asked, turning to me.

I was just about to say Mary, when one of the other girls – one who'd first walked alongside me down the corridor – answered for me.

'Her name's Francesca,' she informed the rest of the table.

The girl's name was Alannah, and she was older and more outspoken than the others. She noticed me cringe at the mention of my new name and laughed out loud.

'You don't like it very much, do you?' she guessed correctly.

I shook my head.

'All right then, let's call you Cisco. How about Cisco Kid?'

The others laughed along with her.

'Yes,' I grinned. 'I much prefer that.'

We were still laughing when a heavily pregnant girl approached the table and put half a dozen hard-boiled eggs on it. Then she brought over a huge plate of bread and butter. I'd always hated eggs, but there wasn't anything else to eat so I decided to fill myself up on bread instead. The friendly chatter soon subsided as everyone began tucking into their food. I wondered what else we'd be given, but no other food arrived. Eggs and bread were all we'd be getting for dinner. After-wards, I was led into a dormitory with seven other girls. Sister Justina stood and pointed out my bed before handing me a basic, grey white cotton nightdress to wear. It was threadbare from being washed a thousand times. Its flimsy fabric was no match for the cold of the room or the night. The bed sheets were also paper-thin, and I shivered as Sister turned out the lights. There was the sound of metal scraping against metal as she locked the dormitory door – our only exit. I heard her foot-steps as she disappeared off down the corridor until she'd gone and there was no sound at all. That was it for the night. We were trapped in that small room like prisoners. Trapped until morning or whenever she saw fit to unlock the door. Although I was sleeping inside a strange room, wearing strange clothes, with half a dozen other girls I didn't know, as soon as my head hit the pillow I fell into a deep sleep. The journey and subsequent work had left me exhausted and thoroughly spent. I could hear girls whispering to one another in the dark but I was too tired to join in.

The following day, we were awoken bright and early by the sound of Sister Justina's footsteps inside the room. Without warning, she flicked on the main dormitory light and ordered us to get up and get dressed. I followed the others, made my bed, and placed my nightdress under the pillow. I was starving hungry and really looking forward to breakfast, but to my dismay I discovered that we were expected to work for an hour and then attend Mass before we were allowed to eat. Instead of cotton wool balls, I was led to a smaller sitting room, where a group of girls were making religious pendants. They were using cheap bits of plastic that held a picture of Our Lady, the Virgin Mary in place. The room was full of girls either making pendants or knitting small woollen outfits for newborn babies. I found an empty seat and sat down next to a girl who turned and struck up conversation.

'My mother put me in here,' she whispered as she clicked the knitting needles in her hand. 'How about you?'

'Sister,' I replied. 'Sister put me in here, although my mother agreed with her.'

Another girl, who'd been listening in, butted in on our conversation.

'My dad doesn't even know I'm in here. He thinks I've gone to visit family,' she whispered.

The conversation continued with more and more girls joining in whenever they thought Sister wasn't listening. The girls had all been plucked from their communities and put in Castlepollard to hide their 'shame' and themselves from the rest of society. As unmarried mothers, we'd all been tarred with the same 'shame brush'.

'How long do you think I'll have to stay here?' I asked the first girl.

'Until your baby is born and it's been weaned. Once it's eating solid food the nuns will take it and put it up for adoption. That's when they'll let you leave, but not until then.'

I gasped because I had at least another four months to go until the birth. Then I'd have to learn how to look after and feed my baby.

'But what then? What happens once it's eating solid food?'

'That depends on if your family agree to take you back,' she whispered in between the click of knitting needles. 'Also, the clever girls get out of here quicker because their children are adopted much faster.'

'Why's that?'

The girl put down her knitting needles and sighed as though it should be obvious. 'Because clever mums have clever children, and people want to adopt clever babies.'

She sat up in her chair and pointed out a fair-haired girl sat over in the corner. 'See Bronagh, over there?'

I glanced over and nodded.

'Well, she's a teacher, but her family don't even know she's here. And look, see Alannah, over there?'

I turned in my seat to see the older girl – the one who'd called me Cisco Kid at the table the night before. Alannah, who was in her twenties, was tall and striking, with long blonde hair that made her look Scandinavian. If she wasn't pregnant, you would have thought she was a model from the pages of a women's magazine.

'Alannah's a nurse but no one knows she's here. Most girls don't tell their families if they don't have to. Those who do… well…' her voice went so quiet that I had to strain to hear the last part. 'Well, they don't always welcome them back afterwards, if you know what I mean.'

I thought of Mum and shuddered. Surely she wouldn't just abandon me here? I couldn't be sure.

'But what if your family don't welcome you back?'

The girl shifted uneasily in her seat.

'Well, that's when you end up like Bridget.'

'Who's Bridget?' I asked, leaning forward. I was desperate to know because deep down I didn't trust my mother.

'The old lady. The one who works in the kitchen?'

I gasped because I knew exactly who she meant. I'd seen her – the middle-aged woman in the kitchen. She'd seemed so out of place alongside the other young girls.

'You mean she was once just like us?'

The girl nodded grimly.

'Yes, but no one wanted her, so the nuns kept her here to help out.'

I shuddered again and vowed to try my best to make sure Mum took me back, but more importantly, that she took me with her to live with Dad in America.

After a few days, I was told I'd been moved from making pendants to sluicing nappies instead. It struck me as being a bit of an odd job because up until then I'd not seen a single baby.

'You need to collect them all, clean them in the sluice room, and take them to the laundry,' Sister Benedicta told me.

I nodded my head to show that I understood. I was too frightened to stand and argue or ask questions.

The following morning, I rose at six o'clock and headed into the main hallway. I had to collect dirty nappies from the top middle and bottom floors, where the babies were kept. But the nappies were heavy, so I laid a sheet on the ground and filled up the middle of it. I carried the stinking pile to the sluice room, where I had to rinse the ones that had been defecated on under a cold running tap. Badly soiled nappies were then left to soak in a strong solution to try and get the stains out. My job wasn't for the faint-hearted. I was used to cleaning up after Mrs Lafferty's boys and my siblings, but that was nothing in comparison to having to rinse and wring out 200 nappies by hand. The half-clean nappies – now heavy and sodden with water – had to be loaded back into the sheet and carried a quarter of a mile to the laundry. I was unable to lift them single-handedly, so I asked another girl to help me.

'This is hard work,' I remarked as I wiped my brow. We paused, stopping for a rest as we placed the dripping bundle on the ground.

'It's one of the worst jobs here, and that's saying something,' she remarked.

As if the work wasn't gruelling enough, I only had an hour to complete the job because I had to be back by seven o'clock sharp for morning Mass. Breakfast followed around eight, or whenever the priest had decided he'd finished his damning lecture of the 50 or so Castlepollard unmarried mothers. And so it continued – a daily grind of hard work, scarce food, and a cold, locked bedroom at night. I felt like a prisoner, but then I realised prisoners had more freedom than we did. After all, at least they were allowed visitors, which, to my knowledge, we were not. Instead, we were locked away – out of mind and out of sight.

I'd been at Castlepollard for a week when my name was called to go and see the nurse.

'I need a water sample,' she said, thrusting a clear glass into my hand.

The glass had a fabric plaster stretched across the front of it with the name 'Francesca' written in black ink. I went into a room next door where the bedpans were kept so that I could provide her with one. The nurse had instructed me to give a mid-stream urine sample. As I entered the room I met another woman, in her late forties, who'd been asked to do the same.

'Hello, what's your name?'

'Mar— Francesca,' I said, correcting myself.

'Mine's Sylvia. I've just had my baby, but I can see you still need to give birth to yours…' she said, looking down at my stomach.

'What did you have? A boy or a girl?'

Sylvia's face broke into a huge smile.

'A beautiful baby boy.'

'But where is he?'

She lifted a hand and pointed upwards.

'He's in the nursery, but I get to feed him.'

I was horrified. Sylvia was a new mum, but she didn't have her baby. In fact, when I thought about it I'd not seen a single girl walking around with her baby. They were all kept in the upstairs nursery.

The 'sample' room was tiny. Behind the door there was a station where the bedpans were sluiced out. On the left were a set of shelves where other girls had already put their urine samples. I went to place mine on the shelf with Sylvia. As we did so, she lifted herself up onto her tiptoes and pulled away a cloth covering three white enamel bowls. Sylvia was much taller so she could see, but as she peered inside, her face paled.

'What? What is it?' I asked.

'Look, Cisco. Have a look,' she said, pointing up at it. But I was short and there was no way I could see.

Sylvia checked over each shoulder, she lifted a hand, removed the bowl from the shelf, and put it down on the side.

'Go on, peek. I'll keep a lookout.'

I peeled away the cloth and reeled back in horror when I saw the bloodied contents inside. I started to scream until soon I couldn't stop. Sylvia panicked, covered the bedpan back over, and put it up on the shelf. But it was already too late. My cries had alerted Nurse Smith, who came dashing in. Nurse Smith was small and fat. She wore little round glasses on her face that made her look a bit like Benny Hill.

'Whatever the—' she gasped as she came flying through the door. 'Francesca, what's the matter with you?'

Nurse Smith was looking straight at me but I couldn't tell her what I'd seen because I didn't want to get Sylvia into trouble.

'Have you got pains?' she asked, beginning to check me over.

I shook my head.

'You come with me,' she said, grabbing my arm.

I refused to move.

'You need to come with me. You need a tablet to calm you down.'

'No, I'm not taking no medicine from you,' I said defiantly.

'Very well, but what's wrong with you, and why are you screaming?'

I pointed up at the bowl on the top shelf.

'Why is someone's guts in there?'

I couldn't help it, I needed to know.

Nurse Smith had been concerned but now she was just plain annoyed.

'Why? Were you looking?' she demanded.

I didn't reply.

'Anyway,' she said, tugging at the sleeves of her red cardigan, 'it's not someone's guts. When you have a baby that's what comes out after the baby. Besides, you had no business touching it.'

'All I could see was guts.'

Nurse Smith had just begun to scold me when she realised, by height alone, that Sylvia must've been involved.

Three or four babies had been born the previous night, including a set of twins, but now I'd seen the bowl I was convinced that one of the mothers must have had her insides fall out. It'd looked like a bowl of chopped liver.

'What business was it of yours to look in the first place, Sylvia?' Nurse Smith asked, picking on my new friend.

Sylvia shrugged and looked down.

'Did you look, Francesca?' the nurse asked.

I wasn't frightened of her so I replied truthfully.

'Yes, and I saw guts.'

'Well, I think you need to come and see me again.'

It was said as more of a threat than a request.

After that day I was terrified of giving birth – of pushing my insides out into a hospital bowl.

I was heading back to the laundry one day when a nun stopped me in the corridor. She had a letter for me. I looked at it but didn't recognise the handwriting. I wondered if it was Mum or Dad, writing to get me out of here. Yes, I thought, my heart lifting, that's it. Mum had changed her mind and wanted me and the baby back home. My heart was in my mouth as I tore open the envelope urgently with my index finger. Inside was a single folded sheet of paper and a ten-shilling note. My eyes scoured the letter, looking for a name, and that's when I saw it: 'Peggy'. I was confused. Why would Aunt Peggy – Mum's sister – be sending me a letter?

Wiping my hands against my dress, I moved over to a corner so that I could read it in peace.

*Dear Mary,*

*I am writing to tell you that your mother has left for America to join your father. She has taken all your brothers and sisters with her. You are no longer wanted here in Ballina. Due to the condition that you now find yourself in, I have to*

*let you know that you are dead to the family. You*
*are now on your own.*
   *Goodbye,*
   *Peggy*

Tears blurred my eyes as I read the letter over and over again. I was on my own. Mum had gone, and now I had no one. They were all together but they had left me behind. I looked for a date. The letter was dated November 1967. I'd been in Castlepollard just over six weeks, yet my whole family had gone. She'd taken them all, and I wondered if and when I'd ever see them again. Suddenly, I began to shake and soon I couldn't stop. I was 16 years old, but my mother – my own flesh and blood – had abandoned me to my fate in the hellhole that was Castlepollard. She'd travelled to the other side of the world to be with my father. I shook my head as shock began to set in. What would she tell Dad? Would she tell him I was dead? Probably, I thought bitterly. I looked down at the crumpled ten-shilling note in my hand that Aunt Peggy had enclosed. Was that all I was worth? Was that expected to set me up in a new life with my baby? It was nothing but blood money. Money that said, sling your hook, you're on your own. Shock was soon overtaken by anger. Holding the letter in both hands, I ripped both it and the ten-shilling note into tiny pieces. I hated my mother and I decided that I would never forgive her.

The following weeks passed by in a blur. I'd resigned myself to the fact I'd probably be stuck in Castlepollard for ever, never able to leave. I thought of Bridget, the old woman who worked in the kitchen, and shuddered.

Maybe that'd be me in a few years. But what about my baby? Without family to help, where would we end up? They'd already mentioned adoption, but I shook the thought from my head. Unlike some of the other girls, I refused to believe that could happen to me, because I was determined that I'd keep my baby.

A few months later, I started to struggle to lift the dirty nappies into the sluice room.

'It's my back,' I complained to Sister Benedicta. 'I can't lift it any more. I just can't.'

Sister had seemed far from impressed, but I was adamant. I was eight months pregnant and I struggled to get up and downstairs, never mind lift a sheet full of rancid, stinking nappies. With nothing else for it, she placed me on laundry duties, where I was told to iron sheets and pillow slips using metal irons that were heated in an oven. I'd have to remove the irons using a thick piece of cotton gauze wrapped around the handle, being careful not to burn my hand. Then I'd have to spit on them to make sure they were hot enough, but not too hot that they'd burn the sheets. It was hot and exhausting work, with a typical day stretching from 8.30 in the morning until five o'clock.

The days passed by with hours of drudgery and back-breaking work until one morning, when I was called, along with a dozen other girls, to see Nurse Smith. As I joined the end of the queue I wondered what on earth she needed to see me for.

'Why does she want to see so many of us?' I asked the girl standing in front of me.

She turned to face me with a look of complete surprise. 'Why? Haven't you been here before?'

I shook my head, so she explained. 'Before you have a baby, Nurse Smith shaves you down below with a razor blade.'

Now it was my turn to be shocked. 'She *does*?'

The girl nodded. I waited for her to burst out laughing, but she was deadly serious. As I glanced up I realised someone else had just gone into the room – I was one step closer to Nurse Smith and her razor blade.

'The worst thing is she never changes the blade. Not once. All she does is dip it in hot water after she's shaved the last girl.'

I gulped a wave of nausea that had risen up at the back of my throat.

'You mean she uses the same razor every time?'

'Yes, and it's usually blunt by the time it gets to the last person.'

I looked behind me and realised I was that last person. One by one, each girl was called into the room until soon enough it was my turn.

'Francesca,' Nurse Smith called out.

I thought of the bedpan of chopped liver as I eyed the glinting edge of the cut-throat razor in her hand. I shook my head but I couldn't get rid of the image.

'Lie down on the bed and remove your underwear,' Nurse Smith instructed.

I felt sick as I unbuttoned my dress. I wondered if she was still annoyed at me for looking inside the pan in the sluice room – the time I'd screamed so loud that she'd come running in.

'Lie down on the bed,' she repeated.

I did as she said. As she slowly approached with the razor in her hand, she noticed me wince slightly. Nurse Smith seemed absolutely ancient to a girl my age. Aged around 65, her hair was an old-fashioned mass of tight dark grey curls that made her head look a bit like a blackened cauliflower. I winced again as she closed in towards me and rested the razor against the delicate skin between my legs. She began to shave my pubic hair as I squirmed beneath her touch. Sharp metal dragged against my skin, leaving it raw to the touch.

'If you don't hold still it'll only hurt more,' she said, smirking.

Her head bobbed up and down as she worked slowly, applying more and more pressure. I remained silent – mute with fear – and as I glanced at her face, I noticed that she was smiling.

She's actually enjoying this, I thought to myself.

And she was. She was enjoying my pain and fear. I knew it because the more I squirmed underneath her, the more pressure she applied. Tears pricked at the back of my eyes, but I refused to let her see because I knew that she wanted me to be scared – to be scared of her and the power she held. She'd just managed to strip away every last ounce of dignity I had. She'd wanted to punish me, just like the others. In her eyes, I'd brought this on myself, and now, with my family gone, there was no one left to help me escape.

# CHAPTER 6

## Giving Birth and Going Blind

I'd been working in the laundry for two long weeks. It was hot and tiring work, and although I was almost nine months pregnant, I was still expected to scrub and wax the floor three times a week. The same floor also had to be buffed every single day to such a high shine that Sister Visitation could see her face in it. Castlepollard had no electric machinery so it had to be buffed using elbow grease alone. The nuns would make us get down on our hands and knees to do it.

I was only a week or so off my due date when I suddenly began to feel unwell. It was the beginning of 1968, Christmas had passed – not that we'd marked it because it'd been treated the same as every other day. There were no frivolities, no presents, just worship. I went to find Sister Justina.

'I don't feel well.'

'Well, if you're not well, then you must go and see Nurse Smith.'

I was nervous approaching Nurse Smith because after the shaving incident she gave me the creeps. But she was surprisingly pleasant and asked me to provide another urine sample. As soon as I handed it back and she checked it, I realised that something was wrong.

'Roll up your sleeve. I need to take your blood pressure,' she said urgently.

But Nurse Smith still hadn't seemed satisfied. Instead, she dispatched me off to a small bedroom.

'Bed rest for you,' she ordered, leaving the room.

I should've felt relieved – glad of the rest – but her concern had unnerved me. Nurse Smith wasn't known for her compassion, so whatever that sample had revealed, it hadn't been good. Afterwards, I was told to provide urine samples several times a day. Fed on a diet of boiled eggs and bread, Nurse Smith informed me that I'd have to lie in bed for two weeks. It felt like being a child all over again when I'd spent months in a hospital bed with my damaged leg.

My new bedroom was on the middle floor. I knew from my days collecting filthy and stinking nappies that the labour wards were situated on the top floor, so I was almost certain I wasn't in labour. As a country girl from rural Ireland, I had very little knowledge of how babies were born or indeed where they came from. Although, following my relationship with Mickey, I was now able to piece together that particular part of the jigsaw.

After a fortnight of bed rest, and in the early hours of 17 January 1968, I finally went into labour. It was a

Friday morning when I awoke early in agonising pain. As the labour contractions ripped through my body I wondered when the doctor would arrive. I was so naive that I thought he'd remove the baby through my belly button. But over the next few hours I grew up fast. My labour continued into the next day but I was given no sympathy or painkillers. At one point I screamed out for help. Suddenly the door burst open and a nun I'd never seen before came marching into the room.

'Shut up!' she screamed in my face, stunning me into silence.

I was in agony but I was too frightened to cry out after that in case I made things worse for myself. Instead, with every contraction that followed I stuffed a pillow against my mouth to try and muffle my screams. By the Sunday, and after three days of labour, the nuns finally relented and gave me a small turquoise pill. To this day I still don't know what it was, but the tablet made me feel drunk. In a drugged-up stupor I fell out of bed and landed hard against the floor. It took me a while to clamber back to my feet but somehow I managed it. I was terrified that I'd injured my unborn child.

'Please be all right,' I prayed silently as I climbed back into bed and tried to focus. The baby will be here soon, it'll be worth it, I whispered silently inside my head as I writhed in agony.

After what felt like an age, a nun came finally to check on me. Following a quick examination she decided that I was ready to be taken to the delivery room. Yet, in spite of the tablet, I still felt peculiar.

'I really don't feel well,' I insisted.

I looked down at my swollen hands and my equally swollen feet. 'And I've got a terrible headache.'

But the nun wasn't listening or interested in anything I had to say.

'Lots of women give birth. You've brought this on yourself, just you remember that.'

I knew they had little or no sympathy for the girls in here. I'd been told that some nuns would whisper spiteful words in girls' ears as they gave birth. It was all part of their 'punishment' or penance for having a child out of wedlock. They'd whisper things like: 'I hope all this pain was worth your five minutes of fun.'

I'd already decided I didn't want that, so I buried my pain, determined that it wouldn't leak out and give them the satisfaction.

There was a small bed in the middle of the delivery room and some medical cabinets. It was sparsely furnished – a large room but with very little furniture – as though it had a sinister secret it was trying to hide. It looked like the type of place you'd expect to be tortured, not bring life into the world. As I lay there, the nun waited by the door. I'd expected a doctor in a full white gown to come in, but instead Nurse Smith entered the room. As she approached, I subconsciously moved up the bed away from her. I'd been shaved by her and her blunt razor every single week up until now, so I always felt wary when she was around.

'You need an enema to clean you out,' she decided.

I didn't know what an enema was, but it soon became apparent when she roughly inserted a rubber pipe into my bum to 'flush' me out with salty water.

'Here's a bedpan,' she announced following the procedure. 'Use it.'

'But I don't need it,' I replied.

'Well, you will when you give birth to the spawn of Satan,' she sneered, looking down at my pregnant belly. The light glinted off the top of her small spectacles as she turned, making her look evil. 'And when you do give birth you can put "it" in there.'

With that she walked away, laughing to herself.

But the fact was Nurse Smith wasn't any worse than the nuns or the priest. I recalled his poisonous sermons.

'You're all fallen women,' he'd told us. 'You've sowed the seed of Satan. You've been evil and now no one will want you. No one. You are not fit to be in the outside world. You don't deserve to be. You're not fit to breathe the same air as decent people. You are nothing.'

I recalled how the nuns had looked up at him in awe as though he was God himself. They'd nodded their heads, hanging onto his every word. I decided then that I hated the priest almost as much as I hated the nuns. I was still thinking about them when Nurse Smith came back into the room. I automatically backed away. But my head throbbed with pain, as though it'd been caught up in a vice. Then waves of nausea began to overwhelm me. As the nurse stood by the head of my bed, the walls seemed to bend inwards and close in on each other. Then everything went dark.

'I can't see! I've gone blind!' I called out in a panic.

Nurse Smith didn't reply. She didn't have the chance because everything went quiet and then there was nothing but total darkness. My heart thumped against my ribcage as I blinked, trying to clear the blackness that surrounded me. For a split second I wondered if someone had turned out the light. Then I felt myself falling backwards and away from the dark until there was nothing. No pain, and no room. Just nothingness. I hadn't realised it then, but I'd slipped into unconsciousness. The high blood pressure I'd suffered for weeks, the very symptom Nurse Smith had failed to treat with anything but bed rest, had been pre-eclampsia – a potentially life-threatening condition. When I finally awoke, I had no knowledge of what had happened. My head felt like lead as I tried to lift it off what I assumed was a bed. Although I was conscious, I had no vision. My whole world was still plunged into darkness. As I moved I felt a stinging pain coming from between my legs, and then I remembered – the baby.

'Hello?' I began to cry out in a panic. 'Is anybody there?'

For a moment, I actually wondered if I was dead and if this was what hell felt like. The priest had told us all time and time again that we would go to hell for our wickedness. I wondered if his threats had finally come true.

'H-hello?' I cried again.

There was a waft of air. It brushed against the skin of my arm. My senses were on high alert as my nostrils flared. I could sense someone right next to me.

'You had a little baby yesterday,' a woman's voice said, breaking the silence.

I presumed a nun was standing beside me.

'A baby?' I repeated.

I was too stunned to take the words in. Lifting a hand, I grasped against the darkness to try and work out my surroundings. A plastic curtain stuck against my fingers – the plastic hospital curtain around my bed.

'Who's there?' I said, beginning to panic.

A warm hand brushed mine and clasped it reassuringly as the voice spoke again.

'You had a little girl, Cisco, and she's beautiful. She was born at 6.20 in the evening. You had her last night, you had her on Monday. She's over a day old now, but everyone – the nuns, I mean – thought you weren't going to make it. That you weren't going to pull through...'

I didn't recognise the voice, and because I was blind I couldn't even see where I was. Fear rose up inside.

'Who am I talking to?'

'My name is Maeve, and I'm from Cork.'

'But how come you're here with me?'

'This is a labour ward, Cisco. I'm having a baby. In fact, I'm in labour now,' Maeve said, puffing and panting out air.

'You *are*?'

'Yes,' she gasped.

Maeve told me she was one of the older mums.

'I'm forty, but this is my first baby.'

I tried, but failed, to visualise her in the next bed.

'But I can't see you! Why can't I see you?' I asked with fear rising.

'You went blind, but don't worry because you're going to be all right.'

The truth of the matter was Maeve didn't know for sure whether or not I'd see again. No one did. But at least she was trying her best to make me feel better.

'I had a little girl?' I repeated, my voice sounding disjointed and drugged up.

I could hardly believe it. I was 16 years old, but now I had a child of my own.

'Yes.'

'You mean, I'm a mother?'

'Yes,' Maeve gasped, clutching my hand in hers. 'And I'm so glad you pulled through. We were all praying for you, and your little girl, Cisco, well, she's beautiful.'

'She *is*? You've seen her?' I said, pulling myself up in bed.

'Yes.'

I was desperate to know, but I wanted to see her for myself, not through someone else's eyes. I turned on to my side and tried to focus on Maeve, but it was no good. All I could see was white gauze, as though someone had draped something over my eyes.

'B... b... but how will I see her? I... I... I can't see anything. I can't even see you!'

The enormity of what had happened overwhelmed me and I broke down. Tears began to flow, solid, heavy, and constant. They streamed down my cheeks as I allowed myself a rare moment of self-pity. They dripped from my chin onto my chest, soaking my nightdress.

'Don't cry, Cisco,' Maeve whispered.

'But I don't remember anything, not a thing. I don't remember giving birth or anything. All I remember is Nurse Smith.'

I shuddered at the memory and felt Maeve give my hand a small squeeze.

'They brought in an outsider, Cisco,' she explained. 'They weren't happy, because they never do that. He was a Dr Cother. They must have been really worried to have done that. The nuns don't like outsiders meddling in their business, and we are their business. That's why they keep us locked away. He delivered your baby using forceps.'

'Forceps?'

'Yes, you know, where they pull your baby out of you. That's why you'll feel sore down below.'

I winced as I remembered the pain I'd felt when I first awoke. I was confused. I was still groggy from my ordeal, and heaven knows what other drugs they'd given me to pull me through. It was too much to take in all at once. I was a mother, but I was a mother without her sight and her baby. I'd have to wait until feeding time to finally hold my little girl in my arms. I tried to picture her in my mind's eye. I wondered if she'd be fair like me or dark-haired like Mickey. Would she have my button nose, or Mickey's strong, Irish one? Would she even know who I was? A wave of nausea washed over me as a thought came into my head – someone else must have been feeding her because Maeve had said she was over a day old.

'Maeve,' I called out into the darkness.

I prayed she was still there.

'Yes,' she grunted, huffing loudly as another labour contraction gripped her.

'What day is it today?'

'Tuesday. It's Tuesday, Cisco.'

'But I went into the delivery room on Sunday?'

'I know, but you've been unconscious since then, that's why they didn't think you'd pull through. But you have, Cisco, and you'll hold your baby soon.'

'But how will I see her?' I wept. 'I won't be able to see her!'

Soon the old tears had been replaced with new ones. A pitiful sob racked through my body, leaving me gasping for breath. My little girl wasn't with me or here in my arms. I felt a pain so deep that it stole my breath away. There was no visible wound only a huge gaping hole inside my heart where the love for my baby should have been.

Over the days that followed, the other girls on the ward would feed me, take me to the toilet, and talk to me about my little girl.

'She's growing big and strong. You should see her, Cisco, she's beautiful,' one said as she spooned food into my mouth.

I pushed the food away because I had no appetite. I had no hunger, only a longing to see my child and hold her in my arms. My heart ached, but the nuns told me I couldn't see her until my sight had been fully restored. It wasn't until almost a week later when it began to return that I finally got to feed her. There had been no rhyme or reason to it, but Maeve's words had come true. Slowly, the white gauze gave way to shadows, then outlines, and finally, blurred shapes. Slowly, those shapes began to fill with detail. It was as though my brain was trying to colour the world back in.

'I can see!' I gasped one afternoon. I beckoned a nun over to my bedside. 'When will I be able to see my baby?'

The nun stopped in her tracks and came over to my bedside.

'Yes, but how much can you see?'

'I can see you,' I lied, even though she was still a blurry shape. I would have said anything to have seen and held my newborn child.

The nun promised to speak to Sister Justina, and the following day I was led, a little unsteady on my feet but totally focused and determined, to the nursery to meet my baby for the very first time. As soon as someone placed her in my arms I was astonished at how solid and heavy she felt. I'd expected her to be petite and fragile.

'How much did she weigh?' I asked.

A nun said she'd go and check for me.

'She was born weighing seven pounds three ounces, Francesca.'

I smiled because I could tell that she weighed much more than that now. In fact, someone had told me she'd continued to put weight on from the day she was born. Although she felt strangely heavy, I could just about make out her shape. My eyes searched for the finer details but they were still missing. But I didn't care: I finally had her in my arms and that's all that mattered. My baby was seven days old, and in that moment I decided that I didn't care about anything or anyone. She was my world, and as long as she was safe with me then everything would be all right.

'You're not alone any more, little one,' I whispered with my mouth pressed against the soft, downy hair on her head.

I pressed my nose against her scalp and inhaled. She smelled divine – the unmistakably unique and beautiful smell that only a newborn baby has.

'Now that you're mine, I promise no one will ever take you from me again. No one. I'll protect you. I'll protect you because I'm your mother.'

A moment later, the outline robes of a nun flapped around in front of me, bringing me abruptly back into the moment.

'Her bottle. You'll be needing her milk if you want her to grow up healthy and strong.' She pressed what felt like a hard plastic feeding bottle into my hand.

I took the formula milk mixture, sat down, and began to nurse my child. I was a mother, and, for the first time in my life, I felt complete. Someone needed me. I mattered. I wasn't as worthless as the priest and nuns had said because now I was a mother, and no one could take that away from me. I had a child. I'd brought a new life into being – a daughter – and it was up to me to care for her and protect her from the evils of this world.

# CHAPTER 7

## The Cornflake Babies

As she grew stronger, my baby, who I decided to call Catherine, was moved from the newborn nursery into the main one. With my vision fully restored I was able to see her for the first time. She was beautiful, with buttermilk fair hair and my button nose.

As new mothers, we were forbidden from entering the nursery unless it was feeding time. The morning feed was at seven o'clock in the morning, followed by another at ten o'clock. Outside feeding times, we were expected to work as normal, but we'd be called back for the lunchtime feed at two o'clock, with the last one at six o'clock. If Mass overran, we'd miss the morning feed. I hated the priest even more whenever that happened because he knew as well as we did that time with our babies was precious. Sometimes it felt as though he'd done it on purpose just so he could punish us more.

Catherine was moved from the newborn nursery on the top floor to the main middle floor one, where she stayed until she was two months old. Eventually, she was moved again, this time to the bottom floor, along with other babies who had been weaned. Altogether there were 30 to 45 babies at any one time, with more girls arriving weekly. But there were only two girls during Benediction to watch over all the babies, and I often wondered what would happen if there was an emergency. But, it seemed, God and worship came before the well-being of our children. Had there been a fire then the priest and nuns would've probably said it was God's punishment because we'd 'sowed the seed of Satan'.

I'd seen something else, too – a large hardback book. Inside were the names and dates of birth of every single baby born at Castlepollard.

Once a baby had turned six weeks old the nuns would tell the mother to deny him or her milk.

'You must give them solid food. That way they'll grow up to be big and strong.'

When babies were six weeks old, their mothers were given two hard, plastic mugs. One contained porridge and the other contained plain cow's milk. We were told to mix a little milk in with the rough porridge oats to soften them so that the baby could swallow them. But some of the babies were underdeveloped and they had a weak swallow reflex, so instead of absorbing the porridge they'd choke on it. The cries and wails of babies half-choking to death distressed us all, but the nuns were insistent.

'Carry on, and don't stop until all the porridge is gone!'

So many babies vomited that the nuns were forced to put down a large plastic sheet in the middle of the 'feeding room' to catch the sick. Mothers would have to sit on a low-rise stool and feed their children but point their mouths towards the sheet, just in case. That way, those babies that did vomit would do so on to the plastic. It was pitiful to listen to the babies that tried but struggled to digest their food. Instead, they grew weaker and weaker until both they and their mothers stopped coming to feeding time. I never saw the babies or the mothers again, and I still don't know what happened to them. But I suspect a few didn't make it.

In order to help Catherine swallow, I pulled the side of one of the plastic mugs down with my finger to form a makeshift lip. I'd mix in as much milk as they'd allow to try and 'water' down the porridge or rice so that she could swallow it. As soon as the edge of the mug touched her tiny rosebud mouth, I'd squeeze the mixture in so gradually that it was hard to see if it was moving or not. But it was, and slowly she learned how to swallow despite her young age. Sometimes Catherine would vomit like the other babies. It would break my heart and I'd silently curse the nuns, who would stand and watch us force-feeding our babies. But as mothers we were powerless to fight back or argue. Anyone who dared question a nun would receive short, sharp, shrift and would be denied what little precious time we got to spend with our children.

More babies joined our feeding group and the newer ones would gag and vomit. I was lucky with Catherine because she seemed to adapt better than some of the others. There'd be around 10 to 15 babies in the feeding circle at any one time, and they'd stay there until they were three months old. The sound of babies crying and vomiting would often be pierced intermittently by a hammering noise. I couldn't see them, but one of the girls told me it was the sound of men working outside in the grounds. I often wondered what it was they were building that took them so long.

*Bang. Bang. Bang.*

The sound of a hammer echoed through the grounds as it hit yet another nail into goodness knows what.

The newer mothers would often be told to pass their babies over to a more experienced mum so she could teach them how to get their babies to eat solid food. I feared for the babies that couldn't feed or refused to because the nuns had no patience with what they considered 'fussy children'.

'Why do they make us do this?' I asked one of the older girls one afternoon.

I'd reached breaking point. I was sick of the sound of pitiful cries coming from babies who were being force-fed.

'It's to fatten them up,' she explained. 'That way, they'll be ready for adoption much quicker.'

I shook my head in disbelief. 'What? You mean all our babies will be adopted?'

She nodded and I felt my stomach plummet to the floor. I clutched Catherine a little closer to me. The thought of losing her didn't bear thinking about.

'But what if we want to keep them? Surely they can't just take them away?'

The girl fixed me with a blank stare. 'Of course they can, Cisco. They can do whatever the hell they want. They're in charge here, not us.'

'But what about the babies that don't make it? What happens to them?'

She shrugged her shoulders. 'No one knows, but they send their mothers to Wales to work, or to the laundries in Dublin, Galway, or Cork. They use them as unpaid workers. Well, that's unless they've got a skill.'

I held Catherine close because I feared for our future together. 'A skill?'

'Yes, like if you're a typist or work in an office. Do you?'

'Do I what?'

'Work in an office?'

'No, I used to look after children and scrub floors. I worked in a factory once, but that didn't last long.'

The girl considered me with pity. 'Well, unless you've got a skill I suggest you continue to feed your baby well, otherwise, who knows where you'll both end up?'

I shuddered. I knew then I had to do something and fast. I had to hatch a plan to get us both away from Castlepollard.

'So what happens if you're a typist?' I asked. I was desperate to know if it'd make a difference. I wondered if I could learn.

'The nuns get you in the office, filling out forms and suchlike. They get the girls to type letters and sort out the money side of things.'

'Oh.'

I knew then it was pointless. Without training I'd never be able to do that. There was only one thing I could do and that was run away.

Soon my baby was a few months old, and every day I lived in fear that I'd arrive at the nursery and find her gone – taken to be adopted. I offered to work in the main nursery. It housed 16 babies, but it was the only skill I had and I knew that at least that way I'd be able to keep an eye on her. If I was to have a fighting chance of leaving Castlepollard with my daughter, then I'd have to get help and quick. I started in my new position working alongside a lovely, sweet girl called Caitlin. She had given birth to a beautiful baby boy called Aiden. Caitlin adored her little boy and would constantly dote on him. She was only a few years older than me, and together we'd look after our own babies and others under our care in the nursery on the bottom floor.

We'd tend to the babies during the day when their mothers were at work, and hand them over for morning feed, again at lunch, and finally at dinnertime. The morning feeds were rationed to just one because by now all the babies had been fully weaned. They were heavy children who looked much older than they actually were. At 6.30pm, the nuns would come and lock up for the night, sealing the older babies, aged two months and above, inside the nursery for the evening to stop their mothers from sneaking down and visiting them. It didn't matter if a baby was unsettled or upset, the children would be locked in that room until seven o'clock the following morning. Like our dormitories, I often wondered what would happen if a fire broke out. With no spare key to hand, only the one the nuns held, the children would have surely burned to death in their cots. It didn't bear thinking about.

One freezing cold Sunday morning, a heavy snow had fallen outside in the grounds of Castlepollard covering the surrounding fields with a fresh blanket of crisp white snow. It was the height of winter and freezing both inside and outside the mother-and-baby home. Late that morning, I was changing one of the older babies when Caitlin nipped out and over to the kitchenette to tidy up.

'Won't be long. Will you be all right here on your own?' she asked.

I looked around the nursery. Most of the babies were already asleep following their morning feed so I knew I'd have a few hours' grace.

'You go,' I smiled, shooing her away with one hand. 'I'll be fine.'

After she'd left, I busied myself changing a particularly filthy nappy. I was standing there, wiping the baby's bottom, when out of the corner of my eye I saw something flash past the window. Curiosity had gotten the better of me and I moved over to the window and peered through the glass. I rubbed a hand against it to try and clear some condensation that had collected on the inside, and that's when I saw her. It was Deirdre, one of the young mothers, and she was outside alone in the snow. Deirdre looked pensive and half-frozen to death as she peered all around. She was so busy checking that she didn't notice my face at the nursery window. I wondered what she was doing outside when everyone else was in church at Mass, and then I noticed something: she had a small bundle in her arms. Deirdre was carrying her baby son, Andrew. Wrapped in a white nursery blanket, she clutched the poor little mite against her breast as though her life depended on it. Deirdre was well known at Castlepollard for being a bit odd. She was a shy girl who kept herself to herself and refused to mix with the others. Shortly after she'd arrived, she'd given birth to a beautiful baby boy. I thought he was the prettiest baby I'd ever seen, but the nuns were horrified because Andrew had an Asian appearance. Not only had she committed the ultimate sin of having a baby out of wedlock, but she'd given birth to what they had termed back then, a 'foreign' baby.

'Your baby is so beautiful,' I cooed one day in the upstairs nursery. I waggled a finger in front of him and Andrew automatically made a grab for it.

'Who's the father?' I asked by way of conversation.

But Deirdre pulled Andrew away from me protectively and refused to discuss him or reveal his name.

'A spirit,' she said, her eyes wild and frantic. 'His father is a spirit.'

With that, she turned and walked over to the other side of the room.

But now I watched Deirdre outside with her baby. She began to run across the remote field that surrounded the home as the snow continued to fall. Dressed in a short cardigan and thin cotton dress, it was clear that neither she nor Andrew would survive the next few hours, never mind a night outside. I checked the clock on the nursery wall: everyone would still be in Mass, and Caitlin was busy up in the kitchenette. I considered leaving the babies to go and find her. I wanted to tell her about Deirdre because I was worried about her and her baby, but I didn't dare leave the nursery unattended. With very little choice, I sat and I waited. I watched the clock, waiting and fretting with every minute that passed. Every minute Deirdre was out there in thin clothing, running across the frozen fields with baby Andrew. Around ten minutes later, Caitlin walked back in through the door.

'Oh, thank goodness!' I said, running over to her.

Caitlin looked at me a little startled. 'Francesca, what's wrong?'

'It's Deirdre,' I explained, pulling her towards the window and pointing through it. 'I've just seen her heading out over the field. I saw her heading out over the hills with Andrew in her arms.'

Caitlin gasped in horror. 'But it's snowing. She'll freeze to death!'

'I know! Either that or she'll fall over and die out there.'

Caitlin looked as panicked as I felt as we both looked out at the worsening snowstorm. It'd grown so heavy that now it was blowing a blizzard.

'We'd better tell one of the nuns,' I decided.

It went against everything I believed in because I hated the nuns with a passion, but I couldn't have Deirdre or Andrew on my conscience. I'd seen them and I'd seen the worsening storm. There was a very real risk that Deirdre and her baby would die out there. Right now, finding them was the only solution.

'Yes,' Caitlin agreed. 'You're right, we should tell them.'

Half an hour later, the nuns returned from Mass.

I knocked against the window as they passed and beckoned Sister Visitation inside.

'Sister, me and Caitlin... well... we've got something important to tell you.'

Sister was tall and she towered above us, waiting to hear what we had to say. 'What is it, Francesca?'

'It's Deirdre,' Caitlin said, butting in. 'Francesca's seen her heading over the hills.'

Sister's eyes widened with horror. She glanced over my shoulder at the heavy blizzard outside.

I took hold of her arm and led her over towards the window.

'She's out there in this, Sister… and she's got Andrew with her.'

After that, all hell broke loose. A search party of nuns was dispatched to go out and look for Deirdre and her missing child. Caitlin and I spent the rest of the day watching out of the window, waiting for the sight of Deirdre and Andrew being led back to safety. Sadly, she never reappeared.

I checked the clock, waiting and willing her safe return. After an hour or so, Sister Visitation walked back into the nursery.

'Sister, thank goodness,' I said, running over to her. 'Is there any word on Deirdre and Andrew?'

Sister turned to look at me as though I was a piece of dirt. Her top lip curled in disgust as she spoke down to me.

'What did you just say?'

I gulped, and swallowed a deep breath for courage. But I was desperate for news and I had to know that Deirdre was safe.

'Sister,' I said, my voice giving way as my throat dried into a nervous croak. 'Is Deirdre coming back?'

I waited for an answer but instead felt a shooting pain as the back of her hand cracked against the side of my face.

'You'd do well to mind your own business, Francesca. But as you've asked, I will tell you this: you will not see Deirdre or her child again.'

And she was right, I never did.

There were 16 babies in our downstairs nursery and that included a toddler of 13 months. His name was Cornelius. Cornelius's mother Grainne was very close to the nuns and hung on their every word. Grainne had been born albino. With silvery blonde hair and ghost-white skin, her eyes were pink, and she suffered from very poor eyesight. It meant that every time you spoke to her she would stand a few inches from your face and blink constantly. I found it intimidating, but she only did it because it was hard for her to see. At 35 years old, Grainne was one of the older mothers. I don't know if was her age or personality, but she could also be very contrary. Unlike the other mothers who lived in constant fear of losing their children, Grainne refused to believe that her baby would ever be taken from her. To protect him against adoption, she would do everything to charm the nuns and stay in their good books. Amazingly, so far her plan had seemed to work, because Cornelius was the oldest baby in the nursery.

'I'm not parting with my baby, not ever,' she told me one afternoon.

I admired her optimism. I also wondered if she had the right idea, sucking up to the Sisters. After all, Cornelius was still there when others had long gone. But sadly, in many ways, it was as though Grainne had been brainwashed by the Sisters, to the point where she'd become institutionalised. Unlike his mother, Cornelius wasn't albino, but he had blond curly hair and was a beautiful and happy little boy. He'd just started to take his first steps when everything changed.

'What's that noise?' I asked Caitlin one morning as I walked into the room and heard a terrible wailing.

'It's Grainne. They've taken Cornelius.'

I gasped. Of all the babies, I thought he'd be safer than most.

'They *have*?'

The screaming continued until it reached fever pitch. Eventually, the nuns moved Grainne to the convent so that she wouldn't upset the other girls. She stayed at Castlepollard for another couple of days and then, like others before her, she disappeared, never to be seen again.

'If they can take Cornelius, then they can take any of our babies,' I whispered to Caitlin. 'No one is safe.'

There was another girl called Noleen, who could barely walk. Noleen had severe in-growing toenails, but the nuns refused her medical treatment so slowly her toes began to claw together, making it almost impossible for her to stand up. Noleen was a lovely girl, but she had learning difficulties and her baby had been born severely disabled. Nowadays, I'd recognise that same baby as having spina bifida, but back then the weaker and more disabled children were treated even more inhumanely than the others. Each morning, Noleen's baby, Rose, would have her arms slipped into a salmon-coloured body harness that was strapped to the top of her cot. Even though she was only ten months old, the nuns insisted we put her in it and prop her up using a pillow so that she could sit up straight. It made it easier to care for her, but the poor little mite couldn't move because she was strapped up all day inside her cloth tomb. I thought Rose would be safe, but like the babies before her, one day, she was taken. Again, the screaming started early one morning. I arrived at the nursery to find that Rose's bed had been dismantled by the nuns. I can only hope she'd been adopted and hadn't died in the night. Whatever happened, Noleen was inconsolable. Her beautiful baby had gone and now she was childless. Within days, Noleen had disappeared too, only no one knew where.

One day, with all the babies settled in the nursery, the nuns told me and Caitlin to buff the floor outside the nursery. Caitlin got straight to work on her hands and knees in the corridor, but I decided to tackle a strip of floor near the stairwell. I was down on my knees when I spotted a door I'd never seen before. It was around eight steps high and there were a pair of small double doors built in underneath the stairs. I glanced nervously over one shoulder to check the coast was clear before trying the handle. I was astonished when it turned inside my hand. Behind the door was a storage area that had three large cornflake containers – each the size of a small armchair – tucked away in a corner. Curiosity got the better of me and I soon found myself peering inside one of the containers. I saw what I thought looked like confetti, so I dipped a hand into the top of it to take a closer look, and that's when I realised what they were. There were tens of thousands of them – all passport-sized photographs of babies and children up to five or six years old. My heart thudded with sadness as my eyes took in the sad little faces – all lost children, all long gone, packed off to heaven knows where. With shaking hand, I opened up the second large Kellogg's cardboard container. It held exactly the same, different photographs of different children. The third box was the same again. A shudder ran through me as though someone had just stepped on my grave. I realised that all those children had been farmed out to other families. They'd been ripped from the arms of their mothers and given to childless or rich couples. The passport photographs, some with embossed edges, others plain, had told me all I needed to know. These babies and children were no longer here, instead, they'd been shipped across the world like prime cattle. Tears filled my eyes as I closed the top of the third box, shut the door, and went to find my friend.

'Caitlin,' I called, beckoning her over. 'Come here.'

She put down her cloth and came running over.

'What's the matter?' She asked as she scanned my face, now ashen with shock.

'You want to see what I've just found.'

Caitlin looked puzzled. We'd only been polishing floors for ten minutes.

'What?'

'Round there, when I was doing the thing... the polishing, I found some photos. There's a door... underneath the stairs.'

Caitlin looked at me. 'What kind of photos?'

I checked around us to make sure there were no nuns listening in.

'Babies,' I whispered. 'Photos of babies. Thousands of them. They were mainly black-and-white photos, although some were coloured. There were lots of little photographs, like the ones you get on passports.'

Caitlin gasped and put a hand to her mouth. 'But Francesca, who do you think they are?'

I shook my head. 'That's it, I don't know for sure but I think it must be babies who've been here. Here in Castlepollard.'

'What? Like our babies? Babies born who were here?'

I shrugged. 'I haven't a clue.'

And the truth was I didn't.

'But why would they be wanting passport photos of little babies?'

I had my own suspicions but no proof. 'I don't know, but I'm going back to check I've put them back properly. I don't want the nuns knowing I've found them.'

I left my friend standing there, sneaked back over to the storage cupboard, and opened up the door once more. I'd left the boxes exactly where I'd found them. But instead of closing the door I felt the urge to do something. Kneeling down, I opened up the first box again and dipped my hand inside it. I couldn't help it – all those little babies, now gone and most probably forgotten by everyone but their mothers – girls like me. Caitlin was right, they could be our babies, and they could belong to any one of us. Dipping my arm into the huge paper mound, I dug down until my arm was elbow deep. I lifted it back out and, with splayed fingers, I let hundreds of faces slip through them. Each sad little portrait picture slipped through my fingers like confetti.

'The cornflake babies...' I whispered.

I heard a noise and sensed someone standing behind me. I thought it was Caitlin and turned to speak, and then I saw her – it was Sister Visitation.

'What are you doing?' she asked, looking at me and the baby photos.

I gulped down my nerves. I'd just been caught red-handed. Sister Visitation clasped her hands together in front of her as she waited for an explanation but I was lost for words.

'I thought you were supposed to be buffing the floor, not snooping. What on earth do you think you're doing?'

I was rendered mute. The images of all those babies coupled with the shock of Sister finding me had stolen my voice.

'I... I...' I stammered.

It was no good; she knew I'd just seen something I shouldn't have.

SLAP!

Her hand struck me quickly and harshly. My cheek burned hot as though it was on fire. I lifted a hand to try and cover the stinging where she'd hit me. I could still feel the throbbing impact of her hand long after she'd pulled it away.

'If you are found in here again, then you will be punished. Do I make myself clear?'

I nodded dutifully. I didn't dare look back at the cornflake boxes, the pictures of the babies, or even the door. Instead, I scrambled to my feet and bowed my head. I was just so desperate to get out of there and away from her.

'There are places we send girls like you, Francesca. Nosy girls. Girls who have no rights but see fit to stick their noses into other people's business. Girls who are trouble. Do I make myself clear?'

I fixed my eyes on the floor and nodded again. I was terrified I'd be sent to one of the dreaded laundries, and far away from Catherine. I was scared I'd never see my little girl again. I choked back my tears and then spoke.

'Yes, Sister. Sorry, Sister,' I said, curtsying for mercy.

'Very well, now get back to your work and we shall speak no more of what happened here or of what you just saw. Do I make myself clear?'

'Yes, Sister.'

'Good,' she said, slamming the cupboard door closed behind me. 'Now get back to work, and not another word.'

I'd never felt so terrified in my life. With my heart thumping and adrenalin coursing through my veins, I ran back to my cloth, got down on my hands and knees, and scrubbed for all I was worth. The day I finally got out of this place couldn't come a moment too soon.

# CHAPTER 8

## The Escape

The force-feeding of babies continued, but I never forgot about the cornflake babies or their tiny, sad faces that haunted my every waking hour. After what had happened to Grainne and Noleen, I realised I couldn't just sit there waiting for the nuns to take my baby from me. I knew I'd have to run away and get help if I was ever going to stand a fighting chance of getting us both out of Castlepollard. I'd already confided in Caitlin about my plan.

'But what about your baby?'

I felt my heart sink inside. 'I need to get out of here first and get help, and then I'll come back and get her.'

To my 16-year-old mind, this made complete sense. I knew I'd never be able to fight or overrule the nuns because I was still a child. I could tell that Caitlin didn't seem convinced by my plan, but after what had happened to Deirdre, and Grainne with Cornelius, I knew none of us were safe because a baby could be adopted at a moment's notice once they'd been weaned. Time was running out for me and Catherine.

There was an older woman in the mother-and-baby unit called Kerry. Unlike the rest of us, Kerry was a married woman. She was also more than twice my age at

33 years old. Her husband often worked in England, but would spend time with her every visit home before travelling back to England for another year or so. Each time, Kerry would fall pregnant. Even though she was married, the Church had decided that times were hard, and Kerry wasn't cut out to be a mother. With each pregnancy that followed, the priest would call on her. Pregnant, vulnerable, and alone, she'd be persuaded and cajoled by both the priest and nuns to go to Castlepollard to give birth. All Kerry's children had been beautiful, and her latest one – an angelic-haired boy named Peter – was no exception. The Church knew it would easily be able to adopt Kerry's children. Without her husband there to back her up, she had been taken to Castlepollard to give birth to Peter, her fourth child.

'Kerry,' I hissed, trying to attract her attention as I passed by the chapel early one morning. 'I'm getting out of here. Do you want to come with me?'

Although she was a grown woman, Kerry was as trusting and innocent as a child.

'But where will you go?' she asked, wide-eyed.

'To get help. If we get help then we can come back for our babies. Wouldn't you like to take your son home?'

Her eyes suddenly filled with tears at the thought of Peter over in the nursery.

'Yes,' she replied, her voice barely a whisper.

'Then come with me.'

With Kerry in agreement, I immediately felt better. There'd be safety in numbers, and at least together we'd be able to look out for one another. I knew I couldn't take Catherine with me, because my milk had dried up and I wouldn't be able to steal or carry enough formula milk to feed her on the long journey home. Ballina was 95 miles away, and I knew I would barely get myself through the journey without having to worry about my baby.

'We'll come back for our babies, Kerry,' I insisted.

I grabbed her hand in reassurance.

Kerry had worked on the farm, feeding grain to the pheasants. She also cultivated vegetables in a special vegetable plot at Castlepollard. There were around half a dozen girls who worked on the farm, so, unlike myself, I suspected she wouldn't be missed straight away.

One Wednesday afternoon, when all the nuns and the rest of the girls were at Benediction, I decided it was time.

'That's it, I'm not going for Benediction,' I whispered as I passed by her outside.

'Where are you going?' Kerry asked, the hoe resting in her hands.

'I'm off now.'

'What, right now?' she gasped, looking all around us.

'Yes.'

I knew it was now or never. It was already July, and Catherine was six months old and she'd been fully weaned. She was a good eater, so I knew she'd be fine until the time I returned for her.

'Hang on,' Kerry whispered, undoing her apron. 'I'm coming with you.'

With everyone else busy, instead of heading over towards the chapel, we took a detour across one of the adjoining fields. Although it was three o'clock on a warm summer's afternoon, I realised I wasn't dressed for the occasion. The flimsy cotton dress was fine, but I wasn't wearing shoes and my soft inside slippers slipped and sank deep into the boggy marsh as we crossed. Fearing the nuns were hot on our footsteps, we battled on because I was determined to make my hometown before the following dawn. Half an hour into our escape, I was walking ahead of Kerry when I felt my foot slip. I became trapped and then I began to feel as though I was being dragged down.

'Kerry! Quick! I'm trapped in a bog. I'm being sucked under!' I cried out.

Kerry saw me and came dashing over.

'Don't worry, Cisco, I'll get you out,' she said, grabbing both my arms and pulling with all her might.

Kerry was tiny – about four feet 11 inches tall – but that day she had the strength of ten men. She huffed and panted as she began to tug at me. However, the more I struggled, the more the earth seemed to swallow me up.

'Stop moving, you're making it worse! I know it's hard, Cisco, but you've got to trust me.'

Kerry grunted and gave me one last wrench. With a strange plopping sound, I landed hard against the side of the bank like a newborn calf being pulled from its mother.

'Look at the state of me!' I gasped, getting to my feet. My clothes were all muddied and stuck to my skin. 'I'll have to find a stream or something to wash myself off.'

As soon as Kerry's eyes took me in, she began to laugh.

'Yeah, but at least you're alive!' she chortled.

Although I'd initially been shocked, I began to chuckle too. Soon we were both laughing at the state I found myself in. I strolled over towards her to give her a hug.

'I'm only alive, thanks to you.'

'Eek! Get away from me!' she squealed, running away from me and my mud-splattered body.

The afternoon stretched on and we continued to walk, if not a little tentatively, across the marshes. Eventually, we reached a stream. Cupping my hands together, I scooped them in the water and began to rinse away the mud. Afterwards, we continued on foot in our bid for freedom. One field gave way to another until finally we'd reached the main road. It was just after four o'clock when we eventually managed to flag down a passing motorist.

'What are you girls doing out here?' the driver asked, winding down his window. I tried to act normal as he eyed us both with suspicion.

'We've come from Dublin,' I chirped up.

It was a lie, and as a rule I didn't tell lies, but I was desperate to get us both out of there before the nuns descended. The motorist was only travelling ten miles up the road but directed us to the next main road so we could continue our way to Ballina. Throughout the rest of the day, Kerry and I hitched another five or six lifts across the country. We'd travelled into the night, until we finally reached Ballina at 11.45pm. We'd been travelling for almost nine hours.

As Auntie Peggy's letter had said Mum was in America, and with our house rented out, I called on some old neighbours of ours called Mr and Mrs Campbell. I'd grown up alongside their own children – four sons and two daughters. I'd been so much a part of their family that I considered Mrs Campbell a second mother. She lived next door and had always been there for me, ready with a smile and a wave. She was a great baker and would offer me and my siblings' homemade cake or biscuits. I was always made to feel welcome at the Campbell family home, no matter what time of day it was, and often Mrs Campbell would lay an extra place at the dinner table to make sure I'd eaten. She gave me shoes and clothes, anything to keep me smart and help me find my way in life. Mrs Campbell had known everything about me and my family. She'd known about my pregnancy and that I'd been sent away, so I hoped she'd be happy to see me now. Walking around the back of the house, I fumbled in the darkness with my fingers for the backdoor latch. Pressing a hand against it, I realised it was unlocked so

I pushed it open and stepped inside. Mrs Campbell was standing in the kitchen, but she almost got the shock of her life when she saw me standing there with my legs and the hem of my dress caked with a silt-like mud.

'Mary, what on earth...?' she gasped as she came dashing over.

'Hello, Mrs Campbell, I hope you don't mind but I've run away. I've... erm, I've run away from that place.'

She clutched a horrified hand against her chest as she stepped back to take in the full sight of me.

'Mary, are you all right?' She turned me towards the light. 'Look at the state of your clothes!'

'I'm fine. Well, I am now that I'm here and not there.' I turned around and gestured over towards Kerry, who was lurking in the darkness of the doorway. 'Mrs Campbell, I've brought along my friend. She didn't have anywhere else to go, so we ran away together.'

With that, Kerry stepped out of the shadows and into the full light of the kitchen.

'Terry... Terry...' the old lady called upstairs to her husband.

My heart pounded hard against my ribcage. For a moment I wondered if she'd turn me away, even though I knew deep down she wasn't like that.

'Mary Creighton, well, I never!' Terry Campbell exclaimed as he stood in the kitchen doorway. He looked shocked, as though he'd just seen a ghost.

'Well, don't just stand there with your friend, child,' Mrs Campbell said, urging us over towards her. 'Come and sit down next to the fire and warm yourselves. Now tell me, when did you two last eat something?'

Kerry and I smiled at each other. It felt good to be home, so good, in fact, that it was as though I'd never been away. Sitting inside Mrs Campbell's lovely, warm, and welcoming kitchen, my body and mind were finally able to relax. My judgement had been right: the Campbells would never turn me away because they were kind, loving, and decent people.

'Mary, where is your child?' Mrs Campbell asked, snapping me back into the moment.

I turned and watched as she ladled hot broth into a couple of bowls and handed them to us.

'Catherine?' I replied. I glanced up from the steaming hot bowl of soup in my hands. 'She's back at Castlepollard. But don't worry, I'm going back for her. We're both going back for our children, aren't we, Kerry?'

'Yes,' Kerry agreed, before gulping her food down hungrily.

'So, you had a little girl then?' Terry Campbell probed gently.

My face lit up as I remembered my daughter. 'Yes, and you should see her, she's beautiful.'

But as soon as I remembered her my heart began to ache. I wanted my baby there with me.

'That's where I thought you could help,' I said, looking over at them. 'Help me get Catherine out of Castlepollard.'

'Why? What's it like?' Mrs Campbell asked, sitting forward in her chair. 'What kind of place is it?'

I sighed sadly. I didn't know how to begin.

'It's horrible, that's why I ran away. You should see it. They treat us no better than animals, and they make us force-feed our babies until they're sick. Lots of children have disappeared, too. But I don't know where they've gone. No one does.' I stopped to pause for breath. The words were coming out so fast and furious that they'd stolen my breath.

Mrs Campbell looked over at her husband, her face aghast.

'I'm not going back there,' I said, my eyes darting between them, pleading for mercy. 'Please don't make me go back there. I just… I just want to go back to get Catherine so that we can live a normal life.'

Mrs Campbell's mouth hung open in shock as though she couldn't quite believe her own ears.

'Please don't make me go back there,' I begged, my eyes filling with tears. 'If I do, I swear I'll do something bad to myself.'

The threat of suicide hung in the air as the adults looked at each other in astonishment. Kerry remained quiet in the other corner of the room, but her silence spoke volumes, confirming every word I'd just said.

'But I thought the baby was being adopted?' Terry Campbell said, finally breaking the silence between us.

'She will be if I don't get her out of there. Please could you help me? Help me get her out of there?' I pleaded.

Terry looked over at his wife and shrugged.

'Mrs Elroy, the social worker, told me she'd be back for us when Catherine was six weeks old, but it's been six months and there's still no sign of her. That's why I'm scared, Mrs Campbell,' I said, my eyes searching hers, begging her, mother to mother. 'I'm scared they'll take her. You don't know what it's like in there, it's worse than a prison. They take babies from their mothers and they're never seen again.'

There was a moment's silence, and then she spoke.

'Well,' she said, patting her skirt across her knees with the palms of her hands. 'No one's taking you anywhere because you both need to go to bed and get some rest. But I promise you this,' she said, holding her finger aloft as if to make her point, 'I don't want you to worry any more, because we'll help you. We'll help you get your baby out of there.'

She looked over at her husband, who smiled and nodded in agreement, and I felt my heart soar. At last, someone was willing to help us. The nuns couldn't treat us like this, not any more. They couldn't take our children from us because we had rights, and with Mr and Mrs Campbell on our side, we couldn't fail. Everything was going to be all right.

A short while later, when my head hit the pillow I fell straight to sleep. I felt both physically and mentally drained, but it'd been worth it because now I'd escaped Castlepollard. I was free of it and soon Catherine would be, too.

# CHAPTER 9

## The Beating

The following morning, I awoke early. I was confused by my surroundings because I'd expected to wake up in a dormitory full of girls. Instead, I saw Kerry slumbering away in a corner of the kitchen, draped in blankets. It took me a few moments before I remembered we'd escaped. We'd escaped Castlepollard! My heart rose in my chest. I could hardly believe that we were free and here, safe in Mrs Campbell's house.

'Morning, Mary,' she called from upstairs. I heard footsteps, and a moment later she was standing inside the kitchen doorway. 'Did you sleep well?'

I signalled over to Kerry, who was snoring lightly in a chair over in the corner, and Mrs Campbell smiled. I stretched my arms above my head and yawned.

'It was the best night's sleep I've had in months since, well, since I was taken to Castlepollard.'

Mrs Campbell's face fell.

'Now, I don't want you to be worrying yourself because we're going to sort it out, me and Mr Campbell. We're going to help you, we'll help you both.'

I smiled gratefully up at her. 'Thank you.'

I didn't know it at the time, but after we'd absconded, the nuns at Castlepollard had raised the alarm. Discovering two of its mothers had gone missing, a search party had been launched. Once they'd realised we already had a head start, they alerted Sister Seraphina. A few minutes after the Campbells had come downstairs there was loud banging at the front door.

'What the...?' Mr Campbell said, rising up from a chair by the fire.

Mrs Campbell followed her husband out into the passageway and towards the front door.

'Who do you think it is at this hour?' she fretted.

'I have no idea, but I expect we're about to find out.'

He opened the door to reveal two gardai – police – standing there on the doorstep.

'We're looking for two girls who we believe have absconded from a mother-and-baby home in County Westmeath,' one of the officers said, stepping inside.

I heard footsteps behind me and turned to see Kerry standing there, staring straight at the officers. She was so frightened that she turned and ran out of the back door and across the fields.

Mrs Campbell turned and, upon seeing that Kerry had gone, pleaded with me to stay put.

'Don't, child. You'll only make things worse for yourself.'

Before I knew it both officers were inside the house, followed close behind by an elderly nun. As she walked into the light my stomach turned: it was Sister Seraphina. She shot me a disgusted look as she beckoned Mr and Mrs Campbell over into a corner of the room to speak to them in private. I knew in that moment I was doomed. After much discussion, Sister convinced them it would be best all round if I were to return to Castlepollard.

'She's not happy there. The child says she's been mistreated,' Mrs Campbell argued.

But Sister Seraphina refused to listen and instead raised her hand. 'I can assure you that all the girls and women who find themselves in there are adequately cared for.'

The Campbells were strong Catholics, so they felt unable to question the word of a nun. Instead, I was returned to Castlepollard in a police car that had been parked outside their home.

'The poor child hasn't even had any breakfast,' Mrs Campbell tried to reason as I was led like a prisoner to a waiting police car.

The officers insisted they were only following orders and put me in the back seat before climbing into the front. One of them turned a key and the car engine fired into life. I glanced through the window to see Mrs Campbell crying.

'Don't be worrying Mary,' she mouthed through the glass. 'Everything will be all right, trust me.'

I turned away from her because in that moment I wondered if I'd ever trust anyone again.

Although Kerry had bolted, sadly the gardai caught her up a few miles outside Ballina. She was also transported by police car back to Castlepollard that same afternoon.

I'd expected to receive a severe reprimand for running away, but strangely nothing more was said. Instead, I was told to return to the main hallway, where an elderly nun called Sister Elizabeth was waiting for me. She'd recently brought a television into Castlepollard, and it was something she never tired of reminding us.

'What are you going to do to me?' I asked as Sister led me into a side room.

'I'm not going to do anything, Francesca. After all, I was the one who went out of my way for you girls with the television and all,' she said, mentioning it again. It was as though she was expecting a medal for her 'kindness'.

'What's going to happen to me?'

'Nothing. You may return to the nursery to resume your duties.'

Lost for words, I looked at her, unable to believe there would be absolutely no punishment.

'Go on,' she said, shooing me out of the door. 'Go away with you now.'

As I walked in through the nursery door, my eyes scanned the room, looking for Catherine. As soon as I spotted her, my heart melted. I watched my baby's tiny face light up with recognition as I gently lifted her up and held her tightly against me. She stretched out her hand and grabbed one of my fingers, curling hers around it as though she never wanted to let me go. The feeling was mutual.

'Hello, you,' I whispered. 'I told you I'd be back.'

Tears welled in my eyes and dripped down my cheeks as Catherine let go of my finger and stretched and yawned in my arms.

'I'm sorry I didn't get you out of here,' I whispered against the downy hair on her head. 'But I will soon, I promise.'

For a moment, her eyes fixed on mine and I felt a strong connection that only a mother and her child could share. It was as if there was an invisible silver chain linking her heart to mine – an unbreakable bond. I'd waited to be reprimanded for running away, but the fact I received no punishment meant that someone else had to suffer in my place, and that someone was Kerry. On her return, instead of resuming her duties as I had done, poor Kerry was taken into a small side room on the ground floor, where she was beaten black and blue. She had been so petrified by the furious beating that she couldn't speak coherently for days. Instead, her speech became slurred and fragmented, as though she'd been drugged. In the days that followed, I constantly looked out for her. I was desperate to know that she was all right. Eventually, I found her sitting in a side room, shaking uncontrollably. I looked down the corridor to make sure the coast was clear and closed the door behind me.

'Kerry, it's me,' I said, taking the seat next to her. I held her hand in mine but she didn't even look up at me. Instead, she stared blankly at the floor.

I sat there for a moment, her hand in mine, waiting for her to register who I was. When she finally did, she seemed scared to death.

'I... I... I... can-n-n't be seen t-t-t-talking to you, Cisco,' she stammered. 'They-y-y w-w-won't like it.'

Her voice sounded odd and slurred, as though it was trying to wade through treacle.

'Kerry, what did they do to you?' I asked, taking in the deep black bruises that ran from her neck downwards and underneath her dress. Both arms and legs were heavily bruised too.

'They-y-y-y b-b-beat me-e-e...' she mumbled.

'Who beat you?' I asked.

I sat forward in my chair so that my face was inches from hers. I had to know who'd done this to my friend.

'This is really important,' I told her. 'I need to know who did this to you.'

Kerry momentarily lifted her head and looked straight into my eyes.

'T-the n-n-nuns. The nuns did this to m-me...' she said as her whole body began to quiver once more.

I gasped and reeled back in my chair.

'The nuns?'

Kerry's hands shook in her lap and she averted her gaze to the ground.

'Yes. W-w-we can't be seen t-talking.'

'But why? Why can't I talk to you? You're my friend.'

A silent rage boiled up inside me. I was sick of feeling frightened; I was sick of being scared of the very women supposed to be protecting us.

'Kerry, listen to me. If the nuns did this to you, what else did they do?' I asked. It was clear to me that as well as a beating, she'd been given something else. 'It's just you seem very slow today. Your speech is all slurred, and you seem slow in your mind. Did they give you anything else? An injection or something?'

But Kerry refused to answer or even meet my eye. Instead, she turned away like a frightened child who had already said too much.

I hated the nuns for what they'd done to my friend. The fury continued to boil up inside until soon I couldn't control it any longer. Instead, I went to find Sister Elizabeth.

'Why did you beat Kerry?' I demanded, thumping an angry hand against my chest. 'It was my idea to run away, not hers. She didn't deserve what they did to her.'

Sister looked up but didn't say a word. Gathering up her things, she brushed past me and along the corridor.

'You don't understand,' I called after her. 'I persuaded Kerry to go with me.'

I watched as the nun disappeared off into the distance. But I hadn't finished.

'If I got the chance, I'd do it again,' I screamed after her as she turned a corner and then she was gone.

At first I didn't understand why Kerry had received the beating instead of me. It took me a few days before I finally realised it was because she was older, so in the nuns' eyes she was the 'adult' and had deserved the punishment. I was only 16, but for once my age had saved me. But it didn't stop the guilt I felt inside. I knew if it hadn't been for the lovely and brave Kerry, I'd be dead in that bog in a field somewhere. Like the countless mothers who'd passed through Castlepollard before me, I'd have vanished never to be seen again.

# CHAPTER 10

# The Screaming Room

A few weeks after I'd run away, one of the nuns came to find me in the nursery. It was around midday and the mothers had crowded inside the room ready to feed their little ones.

'There are two men waiting to speak with you, Francesca. Follow me,' she instructed.

I was totally puzzled. I didn't have a clue who the men were or what they wanted with me. As we walked along the corridor, I thought better of asking Sister what it was all about. She opened the door and I did a double take when I saw them sitting there – it was the gardai, the ones who'd brought me back from Ballina.

'Mary,' said one, gesturing towards a chair at the table. 'Please take a seat, we'd like to ask you a few questions.'

I was taken aback, but not as much as Sister had looked when he mentioned asking me 'questions'. Although she'd closed the door, I could sense her standing outside in the corridor with her ear pressed up against the door. As one of the unmarried mothers at Castlepollard, I already knew too much.

The gardai seemed interested in the fact that I was in the mother-and-baby home and I'd had a child because I was underage myself.

'How long have you been here, Mary?' one of the officers began, taking out a pen and a notebook from his breast pocket.

I decided I'd tell them nothing but the truth.

'Almost ten months. The social worker said she'd come and get me out after six weeks, but I'm still here, and so is my daughter.'

'And how old is your daughter?'

The questions continued long into the afternoon as, one by one, I answered them all. The policemen even asked who Catherine's father was, and had I been raped?

'I wasn't raped, he was my boyfriend,' I replied.

The officer arched an eyebrow and glanced over at his colleague. It was obvious what he thought of me and of all the women in there.

'And who put you in Castlepollard?'

I looked him directly in the eye, cleared my throat, and then spoke.

'My mother. My mother and a nun called Sister Seraphina, and they've both left me here to rot. My mother has moved to America to be with my father,' I said numbly. 'But I bet he doesn't even know I'm here. He probably thinks I'm dead.'

I still felt bitter towards my mother, but that same bitterness had been numbed by Castlepollard. I realised I was slowly becoming institutionalised. I shuddered as I thought of Bridget, the old lady who worked in the kitchen. Maybe I'd end up in there with her.

'I want to get out,' I told the officers. 'I can't even buy anything because I have no money. I hate it here, that's why I ran away. They treat us so badly... some days I think I'd rather die than stay here.'

The officers raised their eyebrows once more at my sudden and unexpected outburst. But I didn't care; I had nothing to hide. The worst had already happened. The only thing I had left to lose now was my baby.

'Please get me out! Please!' I begged them.

The first officer didn't react; instead, he closed his notebook and thanked me for my time. I was left there as both men stood up and left the room. I'd hoped that by telling the truth something would be done. I waited days, and then the days turned into weeks, but nothing happened. After their visit I lost all hope. If the gardai couldn't help me, then who would?

The following months passed by in a familiar routine. I didn't even see Kerry much. Then one day she disappeared – her beautiful baby boy taken from her like all the others. Although Caitlin was still with me, I couldn't hide my sadness. I wondered what had happened to Kerry. I hoped and prayed she'd find some happiness. After losing four children, she deserved that at the very least.

Soon, Catherine had turned eight months old, and the more she grew, the more my anxiety grew, that someone would come into Castlepollard and take her from me. Each day, I lived with the fear that that day could be the last one I ever got to spend with my baby.

One day, Caitlin and I were cleaning out the linen cupboard when she turned to me.

'Cisco,' she called. Her head bobbed from one side to the other as she checked my ears, 'Have you ever had them pierced?'

I laughed because I'd wondered what she was about to ask me.

'Yes, I had them done ages ago.' I absentmindedly rubbed an earlobe between my finger and thumb. 'But I think they closed up a long time ago.'

'Really? Do you want me to do them for you again?'

I shrugged. 'Yeah, if you want.'

She didn't need to be told twice. With a buzz of excitement, Caitlin turned and grabbed something. At first, I wasn't sure what it was, but as the needle pierced my skin, I certainly felt it.

'Owwww!'

'Shush!' she hissed, putting a finger against my mouth. 'The nuns will hear you!'

I didn't care, my ear was throbbing.

'Owwww!'

Caitlin was looking at me when her face changed.

'Oh no, you're bleeding!' she said, looking around for something to dab it with.

'I'm not surprised. What did you use – a pair of scissors?'

She opened her hand to reveal a large safety pin. 'Sorry, Cisco.'

'It doesn't matter.' I cupped a hand around the wound to try and stop the flow of blood.

'Here's a towel,' she said, holding one up.

I dabbed my earlobe with it, and although it took ages to stem the bleeding, it eventually stopped. I gathered the stained towel into a ball.

'I'll have to hide this,' I said, looking all around for a suitable place. My eyes scanned the linen cupboard, and that's when I spotted it – the top shelf.

No one would think to look up there, I thought.

'You keep a lookout while I stuff this up here,' I told Caitlin as I hoisted myself up.

There were rows of cardboard boxes lined up along the top shelf, but they were so high up we'd never bothered looking inside them. However, now I was up there I decided I wasn't going to miss the opportunity. Pulling back a lid, I peered inside.

'Caitlin,' I whispered down to her.

But she was busy looking out of a crack in the door for passing nuns.

'What? What's wrong?'

'Look what I've just found.'

I held the contents of the box in my hands. There were brand-new romper suits and cardigans – everything a baby would ever need.

'There's loads of them,' I gasped, as I continued to rummage through the boxes.

Caitlin looked up, a little puzzled. 'But if it's all new then why do they keep it up there? Why not use them to dress the babies?'

I shrugged. She was right; it made no sense.

'Search me. But look,' I said, pulling out a beautiful blue cardigan. I threw it down to her. 'You should dress Aiden in that. Why don't you dress him in blue, and I'll dress Catherine in red?'

I found two romper suits and passed them down.

'They can wear these, too.'

Aiden had the bluest eyes I'd ever seen in a baby. He was adorable, with a soft mop of blond hair. Yet, when Caitlin dressed him in the little blue cardigan his eyes looked twice as blue as the sky.

'He looks gorgeous!' I gushed.

Caitlin smiled proudly and hugged him close. She adored her little boy.

In the end, I decided to lift the box of baby clothes down and dress every child in the nursery in the smart new clothes. I reasoned that they deserved to be treated exactly the same. After all, they were babies, and they'd done nothing wrong. Removing their standard issue long, white nightgowns, Caitlin and I changed each and every one of them until we had a nursery full of happy and brightly dressed babies. The sight of them all made my heart sing.

However, later that day when Sister Visitation popped her head through the door she demanded to know where the fancy clothes had come from.

'It was me. I found them over in the cupboard,' I said, stepping forward.

Sister fixed me with a steely glare. 'And who gave you permission?' she demanded to know.

I tapped a hand against my chest. I wasn't frightened because I knew I'd done nothing wrong.

'Myself. I gave myself permission. All the work in here was done, so I shimmied up and got them off the top shelf. They're new clothes, so I thought they must have been handed in – for the babies,' I said, gesturing a hand across the room. 'And these are the only babies here.'

Sister flinched as I said the words.

'Well, you need to take them off because you should have asked permission.'

I was furious. There was no way I was prepared to do that.

'I'm not stripping the babies,' I replied.

But Sister was unwilling to back down. 'You should have had permission.'

I knew that I wouldn't win, so I decided to try a different tack.

'But Sister, where have these clothes come from? If they're not for the babies in the nursery, then who are they for?'

She thought for a moment, turned on her heel, and stormed out of the room and off down the corridor. As she left, I heard her mutter something loud enough for me to hear. 'You are a very nosy girl, Francesca, and one day, it will get you into trouble.'

In spite of what I'd done, nothing more was said and no further action was taken. Caitlin and I continued to work in the ground-floor nursery, where we would change, wash, and care for the older babies. Some were teething, yet the nuns refused to give us medication or anything to help soothe the sore gums of the poor little mites. Instead, the babies were expected to cut their teeth in pain, chewing on whatever we could find. Often, they'd develop a fever, but it'd be left to us to try and soothe them and rock them gently to sleep. The force-feeding of the smaller babies on the next floor up continued. Although we had tried our best to keep on top of things downstairs, with only two of us, and with the children locked in at night, lying in their own urine for up to 12 hours a time, some of them developed terrible nappy rash. A few became so bad that their soft skin would erupt into sores that would bleed through into their nappies. It was never-ending, but we tried our best with very little resources and very little time. We had no baby powder to stop their suffering, but following constant complaints from us, the nuns finally relented and gave us a cement-like cream called Lazers ointment. Even then it didn't arrive until late one night after the office had been locked. Only one nun had the key, and she wasn't around. Instead, we were left with a nursery full of babies screaming out in pain.

I was bewildered by the often callous nature of the older nuns. 'How can they do this, Caitlin? How can they let children suffer like this?'

But Caitlin didn't have any answers. None of us did. The worst thing was it was totally unnecessary. I often wondered whether the nuns let our children suffer to punish us more. It was simply inhumane.

There was a bathroom with four or five baths that were half the size of a normal tub, and a further half a dozen normal ones. But we weren't allowed to bathe the children or babies in them during the whole year I stayed in Castlepollard. I began to wonder why the baths were there and who they were for. There were two nurseries situated on the ground floor. One day, I was told to go and wax and polish the floors of the second nursery by Sister Visitation.

'And make sure they're gleaming, Francesca.'

I picked up a scrubbing brush, cloths, a tin of wax, and walked over. The rooms were never used, to my knowledge, but as I opened the door I couldn't believe what greeted me. Each room had been equipped with dozens of children's toys, from rocking horses to tiny trikes, to dolls and dolls' prams. It was all there, but the children we cared for weren't allowed to play with them because the rooms were strictly out of bounds. With no children inside them, the rooms felt eerie, almost like wandering into a museum after the doors had closed. I could visualise the children and picture the joy on their faces in a room like this, but when I opened my eyes the room felt empty and dead because there were no children. One room had a glass partition that had been adorned with Disney characters, but there were no young faces to stare up at it in wonder. To an outsider, it almost looked as though the children had just abandoned the toys to go outside to play. But I knew the truth: the children who'd once played in that room were never coming back because they'd been shipped out like a commodity.

Not long afterwards, I was on my way to the laundry when I made another discovery. I stumbled upon an outbuilding that had been packed high to the rafters with unused toys. The building was long with steps that led up to it, but there wasn't a handrail for little hands to hold onto. Once again, it was a museum – a room full of toys but with no children allowed to play with them. I was so furious that I told Caitlin what I'd seen.

'What happens to them? What happens to the mothers of those children?'

She glanced over her shoulder and began to whisper. 'I heard the mothers have to stay with their children until they are adopted. The prettiest and cleverest kids go first, but some mums have to stay here until their children are six or seven years old.' I remembered back to my first night at Castlepollard – another expecting mother had told me something similar. 'But that's not all,' Caitlin whispered. 'Have you seen the baby baths?'

'What, the ones that we're not allowed to use for our babies?' I said, recalling the small baths I'd seen previously.

'Yes, those. I don't know how true this is, but I've been told that the only children allowed to use them are the ones who've been adopted and shipped out to America.'

'America?'

'Yes. It's the nuns; they send some of the babies out to childless couples in America.'

I thought of my parents living over in America with my brothers and sisters, forging a whole new life without me. Then I remembered the thousands of passport photographs I'd found in the cornflake containers and shuddered. Babies and toddlers disappeared from Castlepollard on a regular basis. They must be like the cornflake babies, I thought. The missing children – the young faces that haunted my nightmares.

'No!' I gasped.

I envisaged a life stuck inside the hellhole, waiting, like a sitting target, for someone to come and snatch my daughter from me. I shuddered because I couldn't ever imagine letting her go. I didn't realise it then, but the reality was those children hadn't just been adopted, they'd been sold, or rather, the adoptive parents had handed over a 'donation'. But whatever words you used to dress it up in, the bottom line was children had been exchanged for hard cash – notes in envelopes. They'd been sold on like cattle to the highest bidder. It was the stuff of nightmares. However, if I thought that was the worst of it, I was mistaken.

Not long afterwards, Sister Benedicta came looking for Caitlin.

'I'm not feeling very well,' Caitlin insisted.

The truth was Caitlin suffered from heavy periods, and this month had been no exception.

'Cisco,' she whispered over to me, 'could you go? I've got terrible stomach cramps.'

I could tell that Sister wasn't impressed, but she realised someone would have to do her bidding and if Caitlin couldn't do it then it would have to be me.

'Come with me to the front lawn,' she said, pointing towards the door.

I followed her across the ground and into a small isolated building – a type of Portakabin – that I didn't even know existed. The room was sparsely furnished, apart from a delivery bed complete with stirrups that had some tan-coloured leather straps attached to them. There was also a single oxygen tank, a sink, locker and a built-in wardrobe at the back of the room. I'd never seen it before but it was obvious it was somewhere the nuns brought girls to have their babies.

'I want you to gather up the clothes and put them in bags for me,' she instructed before leaving.

I looked around me, and that's when I saw them – tops, skirts, and trousers – different items of girls' and women's clothing. They'd been abandoned and scattered on the floor as though their owners had packed up and left in a rush. Scooping the clothes up into a pile in my arms, I managed to fill three large carrier bags. I wondered who the clothes had belonged to. Then I remembered how Sister Seraphina had stripped me in the nuns' toilet back in Ballina. The clothes, like mine before them, would probably get passed around. A type of clothes bank for fallen and disgraced women.

Later that evening, just after dinner, I found Caitlin and asked her about the Portakabin.

'What?' she gasped. It was quite clear she knew nothing about it.

'I had to pick up lots of girls' clothes, Caitlin. You should have seen it, I couldn't believe it. There was a bed in the middle of a room. It was a delivery bed that had stirrups and leather straps attached. It looked like a torture chamber, not somewhere you'd give birth to a baby.'

I watched as my friend's eyes widened with horror.

'But why would they let mothers give birth outside in a Portakabin?' she gasped.

I shrugged my shoulders.

'I don't know. Maybe it's a screaming room.'

'A screaming room?'

I nodded.

'Yes, maybe it's where they put the mothers who scream or make too much noise, or the ones who are very sick. You're not allowed to scream or make a noise in childbirth – it's all part of the punishment. Maybe it's where they put the mothers they don't think will survive childbirth.'

I tried to piece it together in my mind like a jigsaw. The room had been cold and damp – it was no better than a glorified shed. It staggered belief to think that maybe the nuns took ill and possibly dying women there to give birth. I recalled how Maeve said I'd been given a slim chance of survival during Catherine's birth and how the nuns had called in a doctor from outside. Maybe I'd been moved to the screaming room that night? Maybe I'd given birth to my baby in that horrible little room with its oxygen tank and cold steel stirrups? It was something I'd never know because I'd been unconscious throughout.

# CHAPTER 11

## The Price of freedom

We always knew when a baby would disappear because a strange car would pull up and park outside Castlepollard. We'd be on the lookout for cars through the windows, because cars meant visitors, and visitors meant a baby would soon leave, never to be seen again. If you didn't see the car, the first thing you'd know about it was when you heard the blood-curdling screams of the mother. The mother who'd just had her baby ripped from her arms. It was a pitiful noise that reminded me of the howl of a wounded animal. That's what we were – wounded.

One day, I was sitting in the linen cupboard with Caitlin, sorting out some sheets, when I saw a stranger walk into the nursery. She was holding the hand of a little girl I'd never seen before. The girl was only around five years old, but the woman had seemed more interested in the babies slumbering inside their cots. The woman was small, plain, and unremarkable to look at, but her face lit up whenever she peered inside a cot. I watched through a crack in the door as she got closer and closer to Catherine's crib. I felt my heart hammering inside my chest and my palms sweat with fear. Soon, she was standing at the side of Catherine's cradle. I felt bile rise at the back of my throat as she stretched out her hand towards my baby. A primeval instinct took me over and I pushed the door open wide and marched straight up to her with both hands curled into fists. I'd never known a rage like it.

'Don't be taking my baby,' I barked.

It was a warning, not a request.

The woman looked up startled as Catherine turned in her cot, grinned, and held out both her arms towards me. There was no mistaking that I was her mother. I stayed where I was and stared defiantly at the stranger, who refused to make eye contact.

'Erm, of course not,' she said, immediately withdrawing a gloved hand from my child's cradle. But I remained there until the woman had felt so uncomfortable that she turned to leave. Once she had, I returned to the linen cupboard, where Caitlin was standing open-mouthed.

'Francesca, you need to be careful. You'll get into trouble!'

But I didn't care. No one, no matter how rich or well dressed, was going to take my baby from me.

Almost a week to the day, I went down to the nursery to start work when I heard a familiar blood-curdling scream. I ran out into the corridor to find Caitlin standing there. Her face was ashen and tear-stained, and she was holding her arms out in front of her as though begging for mercy. At first I thought she was in some sort of trouble, but just then the nun turned and

I spotted baby Aiden in her arms. I ran over to Caitlin, who turned towards me. She tried to speak, but her body was racked with sobs.

'What is it, Caitlin? What's wrong?'

'It's Aiden,' she blurted out. 'They're taking him.'

My heart turned to lead inside my chest as a wave of nausea punched me in the stomach. Not Aiden. No, God, please, not Aiden.

I clasped my hands against my face in horror as Caitlin turned back to the nun and began pleading as though for life itself.

'I'll carry him. Please let me carry him. He's my child, please give him to me.'

But the nun was apprehensive. It was as if by her possession alone, Aiden no longer belonged to his mother.

But Caitlin refused to give up.

'Please? Please, Sister. He's my little boy. Please let me carry him to the car.'

It was beyond heartbreaking. Something inside the nun must have softened because, without warning, she handed Aiden back into the arms of his loving mother. With him back inside her arms, Caitlin buried his head against her breastbone and began to wail. She was beyond broken-hearted.

'Come on, Caitlin. They are waiting outside,' the nun said, ushering her towards the door.

Nobody spoke. Instead, we watched from darkened corners as Caitlin and the nun made their way along the long corridor and towards the main entrance. I couldn't begin to imagine the pain Caitlin must have been feeling. Her footsteps were slow and heavy, like those of a condemned woman heading towards the noose. Even when they were outside, I could still hear Caitlin's pitiful cries. I wasn't sure what to do, so I walked back into the nursery, lifted Catherine from her cot, and held her tight in my arms. It was clear no child was safe or considered 'out of bounds'.

Fifteen minutes later, Caitlin was back inside the nursery, her arms empty in the space where Aiden should have been.

I wrapped both my arms around her but she was inconsolable, and there was nothing I or anyone else could say or do to stop her from crying. Her baby had gone. Caitlin crouched on the floor and pulled her knees up to her chest until she was in the foetal position. But just as I thought all the fight had gone from her, she put a hand against her hair and began to pull. She wrapped long strands of hair around her fingers and pulled and pulled, tearing hair clean from her scalp. It was as if she needed to feel physical pain to try and replace the mental torture she was suffering. Soon, a group of girls had crowded around her protectively. We all tried to talk to her, but it was no good – she wasn't listening. She didn't want to; she just wanted her baby boy back.

After an hour or so, Caitlin sobbed until she had no more tears left inside. She'd felt so bereft at losing Aiden that after that day she simply gave up. She didn't want to eat, talk, work, or even live any more.

'I'll never get over it,' she repeated over and over again.

And she never did. A few weeks later, Caitlin, like other mothers before her, returned home without her child. He'd been taken from her, wiped from her life as though he never even existed. But Caitlin never forgot him, nor did I.

'I'll write,' I promised, giving her a hug.

'Do you know my address? It's just that I haven't written it down for you.'

'Not to worry,' I said, tapping a finger against the side of my head, 'it's all in there.'

Then we had one last hug goodbye. I knew Caitlin would never get over losing Aiden, but I wrote to her as promised. I was delighted when I received a couple of letters back. Both said exactly the same thing – how much she missed Aiden. One day I wrote again, but for the first time I heard nothing in return. Then I received a letter, but it wasn't from Caitlin but her mother instead. It read:

*Mary,*
   *Please do not write to my daughter again.*
   *Your letters are not welcome.*

I realised then that I had to accept that Caitlin was out of my life. She'd lost her baby, and now I'd lost my best friend. I wondered how I'd cope without her. I later heard that she ended up marrying Aiden's father. I was thrilled for her – happy she'd escaped the clutches of her mother and the Castlepollard nuns. But I knew she'd never, ever get over losing Aiden. Not ever. It made me feel sad to think of Caitlin and other mothers who had faced the same fate. I was determined that I wouldn't end up like them. I'd do whatever it took to stop me from losing my baby.

Well, almost anything. Some of the Castlepollard mothers realised that if they creeped up to the nuns they'd get 'softer' treatment. I refused because I'd seen too much and had witnessed the pain and suffering they'd inflicted on both mothers and their children. Although I was still a child myself, I knew what they were doing was wrong. This was nothing to do with religion. Religion wouldn't sanction the sale of babies or rip them from their mothers' arms. The nuns' actions couldn't be justified in the name of religion because it was barbaric. I just hoped and prayed I would live long enough to see the day when the wicked women of Sacred Heart were served justice. For those of us who didn't or refused to fall in line, life was tough. Each night, I'd collapse into bed thoroughly exhausted and wake up feeling exactly the same the following morning, ready to do it all over again. It seemed like a never-ending life of drudgery. My only joy was my daughter Catherine and the time I got to spend with her. But with each day that passed, I knew that that could end at any moment. With time running

I reeled back in surprise.

'I can?'

Sister nodded, but I was stunned because it was virtually unknown for a mother to leave Castlepollard with her child.

By now, Catherine was ten months old. I was handed a suitcase of stranger's clothes and some baby outfits.

'You leave today,' Sister Visitation insisted. 'We have a yellow dress for you to wear when you go.'

My mind was still spinning and reeling from the shock. *What's the catch?* I wondered.

But there was none. I'd somehow escaped Castlepollard, and I didn't even know how or why. But the best of it all was I'd be leaving with Catherine.

As I pulled on the yellow dress, I tried to make sense of it all. What had just happened in there? Why me and not Caitlin? Why spare Catherine and not Aiden? There was no rhyme or reason to it, but I didn't dare question Sister because I was getting out, and this time for good. Part of me half-expected to be stopped at the very last moment – to be told there'd been some mistake. It was only when I climbed into the back of a mini-bus parked outside Castlepollard with Catherine in my arms that I believed it was true.

'Where are we going?' I asked the driver suspiciously.

I'd wondered if maybe it had been a trick. But that didn't make sense either. Why would they go to this much trouble to trick me?

'Ballina,' the driver said, breaking my doubts. 'You're going home to Ballina.'

It was clear he knew about as much as I did, so there was little point in asking him more. I was just happy to be with my child and driving away from Castlepollard. As the bus made its way out of the grounds and along the country road, I refused to turn around or look back. I didn't need to. Castlepollard would be imprinted on my brain for the rest of my life. I wondered who had intervened. It hadn't been Mum, or any of my aunts, of that I was sure, but I didn't know anyone else, I reasoned. It was just Catherine and me.

As the bus pulled up outside the Campbells', just two doors away from my old home, they were waiting there to greet me. Mrs Campbell came running over with open arms as soon as I stepped down on to the pavement.

'Welcome home, child,' she said, hugging me with tears in her eyes. I was crying too as I showed her my baby, who was softly slumbering in my arms.

'Meet my daughter. Meet Catherine.'

'Mary, she's beautiful.'

Within hours everything had been sorted. I didn't ask questions as to how and why it'd happened, but the Campbells had prepared a bed for me. Another lady living further down the street had sent up a big Silver Cross pram she had no further use for.

'It'll make the perfect bed for Catherine,' Mrs Campbell said, fussing around my baby girl.

Although they had children of their own – four boys and two girls – the Campbells welcomed us into their family as though we were their own blood, never once asking for anything in return. It was good to feel part of a unit once again, but I never forgot Caitlin, her suffering and loss, or any of the other girls at Castlepollard.

It wasn't until 40 years later that I discovered the truth about my sudden departure from the mother-and-baby home. Unlike my own parents, a carpenter for a father and a stay-at-home mum, the Campbells had always been business people. They had money and therefore the means to buy me and Catherine our freedom, so that's what they did.

One day, when I was well into my fifties, I finally plucked up the courage to ask Mr Campbell about it.

'Terry, you bought me out of that place, didn't you?' I said, looking him straight in the eye.

He smiled wistfully and slowly nodded his head.

'Yes, Mary. It was Mrs Campbell, you see. She never got over the state of you when you'd turned up at our house in the dead of night covered in mud. She had to get you out of there, we both did, and we couldn't rest until we had.'

I never forgot that wonderful family or the kindness they showed me and my daughter in our hour of need.

# CHAPTER 12

A fresh Start

Catherine and I settled well at the Campbells' house, and I even managed to get myself a job working in a plastics factory assembling dolls. I was only paid seven pounds a week, and the hours were long, but Mrs Campbell looked after Catherine for me to help me out. Although I offered her my wages, she refused to take them.

'No, child. They're yours,' she insisted, shoving the money back in my hand and holding her hand over mine. 'You need to save so that you can provide a good future for you both.'

With my freedom and child, for the first time in my life I felt happy. It felt good to have people on my side for once.

One day, Mrs Campbell offered to watch Catherine for me, so I decided to go to the pictures. During the interval, I bought myself an ice lolly and sat down to wait for the rest of the film to begin. I looked up and my mouth fell open, because there, sitting in the little cinema, were five of my siblings. They were with an aunt, so I went over to speak with them. I'd wondered if Mum and Dad had returned from America, but as soon as I approached, my aunt told the children not to speak to me. Instead, she turned her head and looked away, urging them to do the same. It was quite clear that Aunt Peggy's letter about me being dead to the family had extended to everyone, children included. I knew it wasn't their fault, but I was so upset that I ran to the toilet to be sick. Afterwards, I returned to the Campbells. It took me a while, but I discovered that Mum had indeed left for America, taking one of my brothers with her. The other children had been forced into care, but were later taken in by an uncle, my aunt Peggy, and another relative. However, they'd tried to turn my siblings against me. My pregnancy and illegitimate child had left me cast out, never to be allowed back into the family fold again.

I was devastated, but then I remembered my cousin Helen, and how supportive she'd been, writing to me at Castlepollard. I decided to write back to let her know that Catherine and I had managed to escape the clutches of the nuns. I was surprised and delighted when, a few weeks later, Helen wrote back to say her elder sister Andrea was coming over to Ballina to visit some friends.

'She says she will call in to see you,' Helen wrote.

I thought it odd, because I didn't know Andrea very well at all. At 23 years old, she was six years my senior, and so had never bothered with me before. But, I reasoned, at least she was family and, right now, I had no family left to speak of. I'd been staying at the Campbells for around five or six weeks when Andrea knocked at the door. As soon as Mrs Campbell answered it, Andrea had breezed in as though she owned the place.

'I'm here to see Mary,' she announced, perching herself down in one of the chairs by the fire.

Tall, thin, and glamorous, with cascading dark hair that tumbled around her shoulders, Andrea was glamour personified – everything I was not.

In spite of my cousin's rudeness, Mrs Campbell didn't say a word and instead went off into the kitchen to make a pot of tea. As soon as she'd left the room, Andrea beckoned me over to a corner so that we could talk in private.

'Listen, Mary, I won't beat about the bush,' she said, examining her long and perfectly varnished nails, 'I've come to take you and Catherine back to Scotland with me.'

My mouth fell open and I looked up at her in shock. Unlike Castlepollard, I didn't need to be rescued from Ballina. It was my home.

'Why would I be wanting to go to Scotland when I've got a job here? Mrs Campbell's been so good to me, and—'

But Andrea stopped inspecting her nails and put her hand up to quieten me.

'You can get a job over there, Mary. Just pack your job in here, it's that simple. You don't want to stay around here now, do you? At least if you move over to Scotland it'll be a fresh start for you and Catherine. It'll be a new life, and there'll be no one looking at you or judging you. You can leave everything in the past. Think of the baby, think of Catherine.'

I opened my mouth because I wanted to disagree with her, but the more I thought about it, the more I realised she was right. Everyone in Ballina knew my business, particularly Sister Seraphina, who was still hanging about in the background, asking questions about me.

'Maybe you're right,' I said, digesting what she'd just said.

Andrea nodded. 'Good girl, that's because I am.'

Just then Mrs Campbell walked back into the room. 'I've made you both a lovely pot of tea,' she smiled, setting it down on a table.

I felt my heart ache. The Campbells had been so good to me. They'd saved me from Castlepollard, and now here I was, plotting to go off again. To even consider moving to Scotland made me feel like a traitor.

'Anyway, what are you doing on Friday night?' Andrea said, breaking my thoughts. She walked over to the table and chairs and started pouring us both a cup of tea.

'Why?'

Andrea took a biscuit off a plate that Mrs Campbell had brought in for us and bit hard into it. Crumbs spilled from her mouth as she continued to speak. 'It's just that a few of us are going out to a dance, if you'd like to come?'

My heart soared. It'd been so long since I'd gone out I was uncertain I'd even remember how to dance.

'I'd love to,' I beamed, my voice rising with excitement. 'I just need to check Mrs Campbell is happy to watch Catherine for me.'

The following day, after a fitful night's sleep, I walked into work and handed in my notice. I decided that Andrea was right: Catherine and I needed a fresh start and Scotland would be it. Mrs Campbell was upset when I told her I was leaving and it made me feel wretched that I'd hurt her after everything she and her husband had done for me. She didn't try and persuade me to stay though because she said I'd been through hell at Castlepollard, and I was old enough to make my own decisions. She did, however, agree to look after Catherine for the evening so that I could go to the dance. As I walked into the dance hall with Andrea, I felt uneasy. I couldn't put my finger on it, but my gut instinct told me to be careful. Try as I might, I couldn't shake it off.

'I've bought your train ticket,' Andrea grinned. She squeezed my arm excitedly. 'It's all arranged. We leave in the morning.'

My stomach lurched, but I put it down to nerves. After all, I'd be uprooting from one country to another.

Yes, I reasoned, that was it. I was just scared of change. I'd spent so long inside Castlepollard that I was used to being told what to do. What I wasn't used to was having so much freedom. But freedom was good, I told myself, because freedom would allow me to build an exciting future for me and my daughter.

The dance hall was packed, but as I glanced across the room I spotted Davina, an old school friend of mine, sitting in a corner with her boyfriend. Seeing a familiar face immediately made me feel better. I linked my arm through Andrea's and led her over towards my friend. Davina saw us approach and waved her arm, beckoning us over. As soon as we sat down, Davina's boyfriend, Thomas, stood up.

'What would you ladies like to drink? A whiskey, perhaps?'

I giggled because I'd never had an alcoholic drink in my life.

'Yes,' Andrea said, smiling up at him. 'We'd like one each.'

I suddenly felt all grown up, sitting there in a bar with my older cousin, drinking whiskey. I introduced Andrea to Davina, but I could tell by the look on my friend's face that she didn't seem keen. Nothing was said, but, as with Mrs Campbell, Davina was far too polite to make a rude remark about a member of my family. Soon, Thomas had returned to the table with our drinks in his hands. I sipped slowly at mine, and although the whiskey tasted strong, before I knew it my glass was empty.

'Here,' Andrea said, pushing her full glass across the table towards me.

'Don't you want it?' I asked, already feeling a little tipsy.

She shook her head. 'No, I don't like the taste.'

Andrea got up to go to the toilet, so I grabbed her drink and knocked it back.

'Steady!' Thomas laughed, as my head and the room began to spin.

He suddenly leaned forward. 'What does she want?' Thomas asked, gesturing a thumb towards Andrea as she crossed the room to the ladies'.

I shrugged. 'I don't know, but she's my cousin, so she's family.'

Thomas looked down as though there was more he wanted to say but didn't feel able to. 'Just be careful, Mary,' he warned.

I wanted to ask him what he meant, but as soon as he'd said it the moment had gone and then Andrea reappeared at the table. The following morning, she knocked on the door at Mrs Campbell's house to take me and Catherine to the train station. Mrs Campbell walked with us and stood on the platform so she could wave us off.

'Thanks for everything,' I said, wrapping my arms around her and giving her a hug.

'Just look after yourself, child,' she said. Her voice was quivering and her eyes were full of tears. 'And that little girl of yours.'

I waved through the window as the train moved forward and Mrs Campbell slowly became a speck in the distance. As the train lurched, so did my stomach. My first hangover had begun to set in.

'I don't feel very well,' I complained to Andrea.

'Here, give the child to me. I'll mind her,' she insisted, taking her from me.

Soon we'd arrived in Belfast, where we caught a ferry to the west coast of Scotland. The motion of the boat made me feel even worse. I spent most of the journey standing on the deck outside taking deep breaths, trying not to be sick.

'Give me the buggy. I'll walk Catherine for you,' Andrea offered, so I did again.

By the time we'd arrived in Edinburgh it was the early hours of the following morning.

'Is it grassy where you live? Has it got a big garden?' I asked as we made our way through grand streets lit up by the morning dawn.

'No, we live in a tenement flat.'

I was a country girl. I wasn't used to living in a built-up area, so Edinburgh was an alien environment to me. Andrea lived with Helen, her young brother Billy and their mother Marion in a three-bedroom tenement flat. Marion shared a bedroom with her two younger children, so I bunked in with Andrea.

I'd only been there a few weeks when Andrea suggested that I get myself a job. She had a job in a shop, so she thought it only fair that I contribute. I made enquiries and landed myself a position working on the assembly line, packing chocolate boxes. I was paid a good wage for the work – around £20 a week – but Marion took half to pay for my and Catherine's keep. The work was well paid but hard, and the hours long. I soon realised I was missing out on spending time with my baby, so I decided to give it up. Andrea was furious that her family had lost a wage and she was on my back to go out and find another job. I decided that coming to live in Edinburgh had been a huge mistake. Andrea had turned out to be a complete control freak, who thought it was her job to run my life. I'd had enough. So, when a friend offered me a sofa in her bedsit as a temporary measure, I jumped at the chance. There was only one problem – there wasn't enough room for Catherine.

'Don't you worry, I'll look after her,' Marion offered. 'Get yourself sorted, and then you can come and get her.'

It wasn't ideal, but at least it put an end to the arguments with Andrea. I visited my baby every day, but every time I called at the house, Andrea would make me feel so uncomfortable that I felt I was no longer welcome. Her mother, Marion, was in her late forties, and she suffered from terrible women's problems. One morning, I called early, around eight o'clock, to see Catherine as usual, but oddly, when I knocked at the door there was no reply. I began to panic and rang the doorbell constantly, but there was still no answer. I sat on the doorstep wondering what to do, when my mind began to wander with the worst possible scenario.

What if Marion's collapsed and Catherine is in there with her? What if they've both been taken ill?

I tried the doorbells of the other flats, but the whole tenement block seemed to be deserted. Soon, I was frantic with nerves. I had to do something and fast. I strolled down the pavement looking for something to pick the flat's Yale lock with, and that's when I spotted it – a thin piece of wire – curled up on the ground.

'This should do it,' I said, straightening it out with my fingers.

I slid the piece of wire inside the lock and tried to twist it, but instead of the door clicking open, the wire snapped off inside.

'No!'

I put my head in my hands, trying to think what I should do next, when I heard the sound of a buggy approaching from behind. I turned to find Andrea pushing Catherine along in her stroller.

'Andrea, thank goodness!' I said, running down the steps towards her. 'I've been here since eight, but there was no reply. I thought your mother might have taken ill or something...'

I'd expected sympathy, but Andrea seemed extremely frosty towards me.

'She's in the hospital,' she snapped before putting a hand inside her bag to search for her front door key.

'Is she all right? Oh no, that's awful! What a worry for you all. Is there anything I can do?'

But instead of answering, Andrea ignored me and went to put her key in the lock.

'No!' I gasped, putting a hand up to stop her. 'Don't put your key in there.'

For the first time, Andrea turned towards me.

'Why on earth not?'

'There's wire in it. I mean, I tried to pick the lock... when I thought your mother had collapsed inside. Anyway, it doesn't matter. I mean, you'll have to get a locksmith, but don't worry because I'll pay. It's the wire,' I explained. 'It snapped off inside.'

She considered me for a moment as I waited for a barrage of abuse. But she didn't say a word. Instead, she calmly stooped down, took off one of her red and white shoes, and smashed it against a pane of glass at the side of the door. Then she reached an arm inside, undid the lock with her hand, and disappeared off inside. She'd left Catherine out on the step with me, so I grabbed her buggy and followed Andrea inside. But as I walked into the front room, Andrea picked up the phone, dialled a number, and then spoke.

'Hello, police? Yes. There's been a break-in. What? Yes, I'm fine, but I've got the person responsible with me right here now.'

My mouth fell open.

'Andrea,' I gasped as she put down the phone. 'Why did you tell them that?'

She turned her back and refused to speak to me. I wasn't sure what to do because I'd done nothing wrong, so I decided to stay put so I could tell the police it had all been one big misunderstanding. Ten minutes later, they arrived but refused to believe my version of events. Instead, I was arrested, handcuffed, charged, and put on remand in Saughton prison. It had all happened so quickly that my head was still spinning.

'I'm innocent!' I insisted.

'It's all right, hen,' one of the officers smirked. 'You can tell it to the judge.'

I was kept on remand for two weeks. During that time, I was asked to write a letter to the court, so I did. In it I explained everything, from the wire to Andrea removing her shoe and smashing the glass. By the time I appeared back in court, the judge had decided to let me go.

'It seems there has been a misunderstanding, Miss Creighton. You are free to leave this court.'

I was so shocked by what Andrea had done that although my first instinct had been to tear down her door, I decided it'd be better to calm down first. To be honest, I was worried she'd just have me arrested and locked up again. Instead, I sat outside and waited, watching the flat until I was certain she'd left for work.

'She broke the glass herself, Marion, I swear!' I told her mother as soon as she answered the door.

Helen was standing behind her and had heard every word. 'Something's definitely not right,' the young girl guessed correctly.

I wanted to remove Catherine from the house and from Andrea. But I was heavily reliant on friends, sleeping from one sofa to the next, so it was impossible to keep my baby with me.

'You can still visit every day,' Marion suggested. 'I'll care for her until you get a place of your own.'

Looking back, I was naive, but I truly believed the old lady was trying to help me. I trusted her as I'd trusted them all because they were my family. A few weeks later, I was staying with a friend when she suggested we go out for a drink at a nearby bar.

'Come on, it'll be fun, and when was the last time you had some fun, Mary?'

I shrugged my shoulders. 'Okay.'

By now, I was 18 years old, so when an Asian man called Mo chatted me up, I felt extremely flattered. At 40 years old, Mo was more than twice my age but, unlike boys my own age, he treated me like a lady. I'd been starved of love and affection for years, and now I found myself at the centre of it I craved it and found it thoroughly addictive. Soon we were going out together. I was young and foolish, so I fell in love with the first man who showed me love. Sadly, I was still too trusting, despite my experience at Castlepollard. Four months after we'd first met, Mo explained he was going to London to visit his friends. I felt my heart sink because I was completely smitten and I couldn't bear the thought of being parted from him. I'd still been visiting Catherine every day, but now I'd become obsessed with something else – the new man in my life. When Mo asked me to go to London with him, I reasoned it'd only be for a few days.

'I can't be gone long because I have to see my daughter.'

Mo cupped a gentle hand around my face. 'No problem.'

The following day, he drove us down south, where we stayed and partied along with other couples he knew. We spent the weekend staying in fancy flats dotted around London. For the first time in my life I felt like a million dollars. I couldn't believe this older, sophisticated man was interested in me.

'There's someone else I have to see while I'm down here,' Mo told me as the weekend drew to an end.

At first I was worried because I wanted to get back and see Catherine, but Mo insisted it wouldn't take long.

'All right,' I smiled, gripping his hand in mine.

We travelled to a house on the outskirts of London, where a middle-aged Asian man answered the door. His name was Hassan and he was around 50 years old. Hassan owned a house but only lived in one room. The room itself was cluttered and chaotic, with too much furniture, a sealed window, and not enough fresh air. As soon as arrived I felt uncomfortable. Once again, my instinct told me to run. It was the way Hassan looked at me that set my teeth on edge, but then, I reasoned, I was with Mo, so I knew I'd be safe. The two men exchanged pleasantries and began to speak in Urdu, which I didn't understand a word of. Feeling excluded, I glanced around the room looking for a clock because I wondered when we might leave. Suddenly, Mo stood up and shook Hassan's hand. Relieved, I stood up too because I thought we were about to leave.

'No,' Mo insisted. He gestured towards the chair for me to sit back down. 'You're staying here with this man. Hassan is my friend's uncle. You need to stay here. I'll be back soon.'

I looked at Mo and then back at Hassan, my eyes darting between the pair of them.

My senses were suddenly on high alert. Why did I have to stay, and what had the two men just been discussing?

Mo grabbed his coat and headed towards the door.

'But where are you going? How long will you be?' I asked as I ran after him.

I didn't want to be left in a stinking room with a creepy old man that I didn't know. I wanted to leave – to leave with Mo.

'I don't know,' he replied, avoiding eye contact with me. 'Not long. I'll come back for you. Until then you stay here, understand?' By now his voice was raised and, for the first time, I sensed an anger I'd never seen before.

My heart sank as I nodded weakly. I didn't realise it then, but Mo had sold me, just as the nuns had sold the babies at Castlepollard. I was now Hassan's property to do with as he pleased. After a few days, I realised that Mo wasn't coming back anytime soon. With no money and no way of getting back to Scotland and Catherine, I simply gave up. Instead, I complied with everything Hassan asked of me, including sex. I was too frightened to say no. Frightened of what Mo and Hassan might do to me. Still, every day, I would ask Hassan when Mo was coming back for me.

'Next week,' was his constant reply.

But one week merged into the next and there was still no sign. Soon I stopped asking altogether. It was easier that way, easier to accept my fate. That I'd be trapped in London, living with a man I barely knew. I missed Catherine desperately and prayed that Marion was taking good care of her. I cursed myself for being so naive and trusting.

How could I have fallen into the same trap twice? How could I have been tricked again? My only crime was to have been too trusting.

One afternoon, after four months of being held prisoner in Hassan's home, the phone rang. I picked up the receiver to hear Mo's voice. I'd dreamed about this moment for so long, the day he'd get back in touch, but now he had, I wanted to cry.

'Mary, I want you to meet me at the train station.'

'Which one?' I asked, desperate to get away.

Mo told me to meet him in central London, but I had no money and no way of getting there.

'Please come and get me!' I begged, feeling my chance slipping away.

'I'll be there soon.'

But it wasn't until the following day that Mo pulled up in his familiar green Cortina. I ran out to him before Hassan could try and stop me.

'Why did you leave me?' I began to sob. Tears spilled down my cheeks.

'He's my friend,' Mo replied without a hint of remorse.

I turned and stared at him, but somehow it was as though I was seeing him for the first time. Instead of seeing a handsome face, I noticed how harsh it actually was. His eyes seemed cold and hard, and I'd seen them glint with anger the day he'd walked out on me, leaving me to my own fate at Hassan's. I realised then that Mo wasn't the charming older man I'd fallen in love with. He was a crook and a pimp to boot, and I'd just been turned into a prostitute by him.

'Just take me back to Edinburgh, I want to see my child.'

Mo sneered, started up the engine, and we drove off down the road. 'I just need to drop in on someone before we go home.'

Fear caught at the back of my throat, stealing my breath, and my body felt numb. I knew what this meant – he was taking me somewhere else. I desperately wanted to make a run for it – to jump from the car – but then, I knew Mo. I'd seen a different side to him. For the first time, I'd seen anger inside him. This had been no accident, this had all been arranged. I knew then that if I ran, he'd find me and kill me.

If he can pimp you out, he's capable of anything, I thought as London's landmarks passed by in a blur.

An hour or so later, we pulled up outside a flat in central London, where we were met by twin brothers, who were both in their thirties. Once again, Mo left me there. I was held inside the flat for two torturous days, during which time I was forced to have sex with both brothers. By the time he returned for me, I was utterly terrified of him. We left for Edinburgh that night, driving through the night. As the sun began to rise, we pulled up outside an old hotel that had been converted into bedsits.

'I want you to come inside and meet Tariq,' he said, stretching as he climbed out of the car.

My legs felt like lead, and my body felt battered as I forced one foot in front of the other and followed him inside the building. We went into the landlord's quarters, where Tariq was waiting for us.

'Sit down,' Mo barked, so I did as I was told.

The two men chatted before Mo stood up and left the room. Moments later, Tariq grabbed me roughly and threw me down on the bed. But by now I'd had enough and for the first time I started to fight back.

'Get off me!' I said, beating my fists against him as hard as I could.

But it was futile because he was so much stronger than me. Instead, he pinned me down on the bed and brutally raped me. Afterwards, tear-stained and sore, I started to sob as he stood and zipped up his trousers. But then he said something unexpected. 'Stay here. I've heard you've got a baby, so you can have a room and bring your baby.'

My mind felt fragmented, like a broken mirror that had been smashed to smithereens. I knew I couldn't run because Mo would find me and kill me. In the mad warped thing that had now become my life, I reasoned that, although Tariq had raped me, at least he had offered me a room, a place of my own where I could bring Catherine. I could have reported both him and Mo to the police, and for a split second I actually considered it. But I already had a deep mistrust of the police after what had happened in Edinburgh, and I knew they'd never believe me. Besides, rape wasn't as commonly acknowledged then as it is now and they'd just mark me down as a neurotic woman. 'Here,' Tariq said, handing me a piece of paper as I stumbled to my feet to get dressed. 'Go to the Social Security and give them that receipt. They will give you money for a room here.'

I nodded, even though I wasn't sure what I'd just agreed to. Tariq explained that in return for the room, all I'd have to do was empty the electricity meters once a week.

'There are twelve rooms, but you empty the meters and give the money to me. Do you understand?'

'Yes,' I replied, my voice barely a whisper.

'Good. Now, here's the key to your room.'

Although I now had a place of my own, I decided it'd be safer not to bring Catherine back to live there. After that first time, Tariq would often walk into my room and demand sex. I realised it was no environment to bring up a child, even if I did miss her desperately. Instead, I continued to visit her daily.

'Where is it you're living now, Mary?' Marion asked me one day.

I was too ashamed to tell her the truth, so I lied and told her I was staying with a friend. But the more Tariq got to know me, the less demands he made. After a couple of months, he'd stopped demanding sex and we settled into a normal tenant and landlord relationship. With life more normal, I decided it was time to get Catherine and bring her to live with me. Soon, my life had begun to settle down. I'd not seen Mo in a while, but the time apart from him had allowed me to move on. That was until one night when I returned home to find him waiting inside the building.

'Missed me?' he asked.

I was so startled that I almost jumped out of my skin. I glanced over at him, but his eyes were wild and glazed, as though he was high on something – cocaine, I guessed.

'What do you want, Mo?' I said, trying to hide the fear in my voice.

'Aww, now don't be like that. You're my girlfriend, my lady,' he sneered, holding his hands out to me.

But I didn't want to be his girlfriend any more. In fact, I wanted nothing more to do with him.

'It's over, Mo,' I said turning away.

But he refused to listen. I felt a hand grab my arm and twist it high behind my back. I was no match for his strength as he marched me into my room, pinned me down and raped me throughout the long night. Sore and bleeding, I pulled the sheet round me protectively and watched as he lay beside me sleeping soundly. I wanted to take a knife from the kitchen and plunge it straight into his back. I was just grateful that Catherine was so young that she wouldn't remember this or him. I wanted to kill him for what he'd done to me, but I couldn't because my baby needed me. As much as I wanted to punish him, I couldn't do it because I couldn't leave her without a mother. We'd been through too much.

The following day, Mo got up and then left as though nothing had happened. A month or so later when my period was late, I realised that I was pregnant. I felt sick: I was pregnant with the monster's child. I was so trauma-tised that I initially went into denial. If I could pretend it hadn't happened then maybe it wouldn't come true. But as my stomach began to swell, I knew I'd have to do it – I'd have to tell Mo.

'What do you want to see me about?' he asked. He was annoyed that I'd asked to see him and I could tell he was feeling bad-tempered.

'I-I-I'm pregnant,' I replied, blurting the words out before my courage failed me.

He slumped down into a chair as though the stuffing had been knocked from him.

'How? Is it mine?'

'Yes.'

Mo put his head in his hands as he tried to digest the news. 'Well, you can't have it. I'm married, so I can't have a child with you.'

I placed a protective hand across my stomach. It might be his child, but there was no way I was going to lose it. I'd seen too many mothers lose their babies at Castlepollard.

'What do you mean?' I asked, backing away from him warily.

Mo looked up at me for the very first time. His eyes looked as cold and dead as the night he'd raped me. There was no emotion in his voice as he spoke.

'I mean, you will have an abortion.'

# CHAPTER 13

## Running Scared

In spite of my protests, Mo insisted I go to Edinburgh Royal Infirmary to have the abortion.

'You can't have that child,' he said over and over again. 'You just can't. No arguments. You understand?'

I desperately wanted to keep my unborn baby, but Mo had been threatening and I felt far too weak and vulnerable to go against his wishes. It felt like being locked inside Castlepollard all over again, but instead of the nuns, I now had a man trying to control me. They'd wanted to take my baby and so did he. Looking back, I think my time at the mother-and-baby unit had brainwashed me into believing that I wasn't good enough to be a mother. When I'd been pregnant I'd had people constantly telling me that I was a 'fallen woman' and not fit to live in society or even breathe the same air as 'decent people'. They told me I wasn't fit for purpose, never mind motherhood. Although I'd tried to ignore it, somewhere along the line part of it had seeped in until soon I started to believe that maybe I wasn't good enough. After all, I'd had people trying to take Catherine from me from the day she was born and that had continued even after I'd moved to Scotland. I began to question everything. I was weak and extremely vulnerable and, as a single mother, it was my job to protect Catherine. I couldn't put her under any risk from Mo, or what he might do if I disobeyed him.

'I'll come for you tomorrow. Be ready,' he said, closing the door behind him.

That evening I couldn't sleep because I was fearful of what the following day would bring. When Mo arrived early the following morning with his friend Assad and told me to go with them I didn't dare argue. Deep down I knew it was wrong. I wanted to run, but in truth I had nowhere to go. With no other option, I dropped Catherine off at Marion's house and Mo drove me to the hospital.

'You tell them that you want an abortion,' he said, hitting his hand against the steering wheel. 'Just be firm, and whatever you do, don't let them convince you otherwise.'

An abortion went against my Catholic faith and everything I believed in. How could I, even under duress, kill a child?

'You must do it and you will,' said Mo as we walked towards the hospital entrance. I felt a hard shove against my back as he pushed me through the door.

Assad was with us, and I wondered how much he knew and what Mo had told him. Did he even know the child I was about to kill was Mo's?

After speaking to a lady at reception, I was told to wait because a nurse would be with me soon. Eventually, after answering lots of questions, I was led into a room with a doctor.

'Just get this thing out of me,' I begged. 'I'm not ready to have another child. Please help me.'

After a long consultation I managed to convince the staff that having another baby would seriously harm my mental well-being.

'I just don't think I could cope,' I lied.

I dabbed my tear-stained face, all the time thinking of Mo and his friend, who were waiting outside the room.

My heart ached as a nurse led me into a nearby ward. We were walking along the hospital corridor closely followed by Mo and Assad, when she turned to me. 'Would your husband like to come in with you?'

I was just about to explain that Mo wasn't my husband when he stepped in between us. 'Yes, I think I need to be with her,' he said, feigning concern.

I wanted to scream because Mo was a monster. It had been his idea to kill my baby, not mine. But the nurse was kind and led both Mo and Assad on to the ward and over to my hospital bed. After she'd left, they each pulled up a chair and sat down at the side of it. Now I was under guard. I watched as they spoke about business in Urdu, as though this was just another normal day in the office.

They're going to kill my baby, I thought as a solitary tear ran down my face.

My swollen stomach pulled and stretched against the sheet that the nurse had gently laid over the top of me. I knew then that I couldn't do it – I couldn't kill my child. I had to get out of there and away from Mo as soon as possible. I glanced across at him as he chatted with Assad.

'What you looking at?' Mo snapped, breaking into my thoughts.

'Erm, nothing,' I mumbled, my hands trembling at my side.

Assad looked over and smiled. 'You will be soon out of here, Mary,' he said breezily as though killing a child was an everyday occurrence.

I wanted to be out of there, but not without my unborn child. Unsure what to do, I bided my time, waiting long into the afternoon. Although they'd been speaking mainly in Urdu, I caught the odd word of English, and had overheard Mo say something about going away on business.

'When will you be leaving?' I asked.

He looked over at me. 'Soon. In the next few days.'

I knew then what I had to do.

A little while later, both men stood up and turned to leave.

'Where are you going?' I asked, propping myself up in my bed.

'Coffee and a cigarette. Why, do you want anything?'

'No, I'm fine. I'll just wait for the doctor. I think I'll be going down soon anyway – they said they were coming to get me at four, and it's three o'clock now.'

Mo nodded, and then they left. I watched them walk out of the ward and along the corridor until they'd turned the corner and were finally out of sight. With no time to lose, I pulled back the sheet and jumped to my feet. Thankfully, I'd left my own clothes on because I'd refused to change into the hospital gown until the very last minute. Pushing both feet quickly into my shoes, I grabbed my handbag and started to walk as fast as I could. The corridors were a maze but I knew Mo and Assad had headed over towards the cafe, so I turned the opposite way and left the hospital by a different exit to the one we'd come in through. I knew I couldn't return home, so I went to a telephone box and, with a trembling hand, scrambled for change. I waited for the pips, pushed the money into the phone box and spoke to my friend Isla. We'd first met when she visited a friend who rented a room in the same house as me. Unlike my housemate, I'd taken to Isla because she was kind and a good listener. After that, we'd quickly become good friends.

'Isla, thank God!' I said as soon as she picked up the phone. 'Can I come and stay with you? I need to lie low for a while. I'll explain everything when I get there.'

Isla sounded shocked but told me to come straight over.

'I'm pregnant,' I blurted out as soon as she'd opened the door. 'Mo's had me at the hospital. He wants me to have an abortion, but that's the last thing I want,' I said, falling into her arms.

Isla invited me in, made me a mug of strong tea, and sat me down. She listened in horror with her hand to her mouth as I recounted the whole sorry saga.

'You need to stay away from him, Mary. Stay here as long as you want, but promise me you'll stay away from him.'

'Yes,' I said, sipping at the mug of tea. 'I will.'

I was almost four months pregnant, but I stayed at Isla's for another month to be sure that Mo had left the country. In spite of what had happened, I asked Marion if she'd mind Catherine for me because I was terrified Mo would find me and hurt us both. But as more time passed, word got back to me that he'd left Scotland.

'Are you sure you'll be all right? You can stay for as long as you want?' Isla offered as I packed up my things.

I shook my head. 'No, you've done more than enough for me. I really don't know what I would've done without you,' I said, hugging her goodbye.

I left and returned to my bedsit. With Mo gone, I was finally able to relax and enjoy the rest of my pregnancy. On 29 June 1970, I gave birth to a beautiful baby girl, who I called Rabiya, which means queen or princess. Rabiya weighed a healthy 7oz 6lb, and as soon as I held her in my arms, I knew I'd done the right thing.

I'd seen nothing of Andrea for months. However, when I opened my eyes only hours after the birth I sensed someone sitting beside me, watching me. I instinctively knew it was her. I was scared she'd come for my baby, just as she'd done with Catherine. But as my gaze fell down towards her stomach I realised she had a secret of her own – she was pregnant. Somehow, it made me feel more secure. If she was expecting her own then she wouldn't want to take mine from me.

'Where's the baby, Mary. Can I see her?' Andrea asked.

I waited for her to mention her own pregnancy, but as soon as she caught me looking at her swollen stomach she covered herself self-consciously with her arms.

'She's over here,' I said, getting up out of bed. 'They've put her in the nursery.'

We walked the length of the ward to a small room at the top. Peering through the window, I watched as Andrea's eyes scanned the babies inside.

'Which one is she?'

'That one,' I said proudly. I lifted my hand and pointed out my little girl. 'Isn't she beautiful?'

Andrea's eyes fell upon Rabiya.

'Yes, she's nice,' she sniffed, before walking away from the window.

I knew that she judged me because of the colour of my baby. Others did, too. It was 1970. People were ignorant and racism was rife, but I didn't care. I loved my baby, and I vowed that nothing or no one would ever take her away from me. I left hospital with Rabiya in my arms a week or so later. I felt complete. I had two girls that I adored, and although my life was far from perfect I was determined to give them the kind of life I'd never had. Marion had offered to look after Catherine while I'd been in hospital, and she was thrilled when I showed her Rabiya.

'She's beautiful, Mary.'

One day, I was outside pushing Rabiya along in her pram when I bumped into Andrea's boyfriend, Andrew. I'd only met him a few times, but he was a lovely fella. I'd been told by Marion that they'd got married and Andrea had given birth to a little boy.

'Congratulations,' I said as he approached the pram and peered inside to see my new baby. 'I'd heard Andrea had a baby. You must be so excited, especially with it being your first child and all.'

Andrew straightened up, and I watched as his face clouded over. He looked far from a besotted new father.

'You don't know what I've been through, Mary,' Andrew began. 'She tried everything to get rid of it even though I wanted to keep it. In the end we got married, but only because she couldn't find another way out.'

A cold shiver ran down my spine. Andrea really was the cold and calculating bitch I'd always had her down to be. At least now she had her own baby to keep her busy so she'd leave me alone.

I returned home with Rabiya, taking her and Catherine back to my bedsit. Tariq, my landlord, took one look at my newborn baby and his heart melted. A few hours later, he knocked at my door.

'Mary,' he said, standing there awkwardly in the doorway. 'I just want to say that I'm, erm, well, I'm sorry. Sorry for what I did to you. I mean, it wasn't right.'

I looked at him blankly and then I realised, he was apologising for the rape.

'Sorry for what I did to you when you first came here,' he explained. 'You're a good person, Mary, and a good mother. You have my word that it won't happen again, and you can stay here rent-free from now on.'

Tariq didn't say it, but I think he felt sorry for me. Now that I had Mo's child, he realised what I'd been through. In spite of what he'd done when we'd first met, at least he was trying to help me back on my feet, unlike Mo. However, now that he knew, news spread quickly. It soon reached Mo that I'd given birth to a little girl, and within days he was knocking on my door. I immediately went to Rabiya. My heart was thumping hard against my ribs because I was convinced he was there to hurt her, me, or us both. But I was wrong.

'I've come to see her,' he said with a gentleness I'd never heard before.

'She's tired,' I said warily, but Mo refused to listen and barged his way in.

Instead of anger, he began fussing over his little girl, slipping into the role of a doting dad with natural ease. Shortly afterwards, the door opened again and Tariq stepped into my room.

'Everything all right in here?' he asked, eyeing Mo suspiciously. He didn't say it, but he didn't have to: Tariq was letting me know that he was keeping an eye on me.

I looked over at Mo, cooing over the baby he'd wanted to abort only a few months earlier, and I felt my blood boil. I ran over towards him and tore her from his arms.

'Get away from Rabiya!' I roared like a lioness trying to protect her young cub. 'She's nothing to do with you.'

Mo turned sharply and I noticed that his face had changed. The softness he'd shown towards his daughter had vanished in an instant. Out of the corner of my eye I watched as he lifted his hand high into the air. Seconds later, he'd brought it down against the side of my face with a sickening crack.

'Shut up!'

For a split second time stopped. I covered my face with my hand as Mo stood there looking as though he wanted to kill me.

Then a voice broke the silence. 'I think you should leave.'

It was Tariq. He stepped forward and pointed towards the door. I'd expected Mo to react, to turn on Tariq, but instead he left without another word. That day, Mo walked out of my room and out of our lives for ever. For the first time for months I felt as though I could breathe again.

# CHAPTER 14

## The Babysitter

After Mo, I decided I was better off alone because I felt unable to trust anyone, men in particular. When I'd been pregnant with Mo's child I'd met a lovely man called Adam, but because I was wary I decided to keep it on a friendship-only basis. Adam was Scottish and had served in the Army. He was a wonderful man and as far removed from Mo as you could get. But I'd been jilted by Mickey, who had, quite literally, left me holding the baby, so I had very little confidence in myself or relationships. This had been followed by my 'relationship' with Mo. Even my own family had abandoned me, so I felt and believed that I was truly worthless and didn't deserve any better. But Adam was patient, and he gradually began to restore my faith in men. Slowly but surely, our friendship blossomed into a relationship. Even so, I still had the nagging doubt in the back of my mind that I wasn't quite good enough for him. I was used to men treating me badly. Those I'd been with in the past had abandoned me, not held my hand. But Adam was different because he looked after me and my girls. I didn't feel as though I deserved such love, but Isla encouraged me to let down my guard and learn to trust again.

'He's good for you. Adam's a good man. You deserve him, Mary, so go out and have some fun together.'

But however much I wanted the relationship to work, somehow it didn't. I wondered if my deep mistrust of people in general had left me permanently scarred. A short while later, I met another man called John. Unlike Adam, John was controlling and the sort of man I was used to and felt I deserved. It wasn't long before a push became a shove, then a slap, and then a punch. I'd try to keep his violence away from my home and my girls, but John would pursue me and then batter me senseless.

'Paki lover,' he hissed, pointing at Rabiya in her crib.

I hated John, but I'd got myself in a situation where I was far too scared to ask him to leave. Like Adam, John was in the Army, but he was a completely different animal. Once, he beat me so badly that I could barely stand up. That's when I decided I couldn't carry on like this: I had to protect my girls and myself. I picked up the phone, rang his barracks, and asked the military police to remove him from my flat.

'You bitch,' he spat as they led him away.

John soon realised his punishment for beating a woman would be far worse once they'd got him back to the barracks. But I didn't care, I was just relieved to have finally got rid of him.

'That's it, I'm done with men,' I told Isla. 'I just seem to attract the wrong ones. What's wrong with me?'

Isla wrapped a kind arm around my shoulders and gave me a hug. 'Nothing, Mary. There's nothing wrong with you. You deserve better, that's all.'

I knew she was right, but my life had been a roller coaster from the moment the nuns had trapped me inside Castlepollard. I started to wonder if I'd ever be able to enjoy a normal life again.

'What you need is a good night out,' Isla suggested.

So, a few weeks later when a group of girls asked me out, I decided to take them up on it. Sadly, all my girl-friends were either out or unavailable at such short notice. I was about to give up on the idea altogether when Adam rang me.

'How you doing, Mary?'

'I'm a bit fed up, if truth be told,' I admitted.

He asked me what was wrong, so I told him all about my planned night out. 'I can't get a babysitter.'

There was a pause, and then he spoke. 'I'll babysit for you, if you like?'

His offer left me stumped. 'But, you're a man. I mean, wouldn't you mind?'

Adam laughed. 'Mary, I know your girls as well as anyone. Besides, they know me. I'd be more than happy to look after them if it means you can go out with your friends.'

'Let me think about it. I'll ring you back.'

An hour or so later I did.

'Adam, it's me. All right, you're on!'

'Okay,' he chuckled. 'I'll be over in an hour or so.'

'I won't be out late, I promise!'

Adam laughed some more. 'I know!'

Pulling on a dress and applying some lipstick, I thought how lucky I was to have a friend like Adam. He was such a nice fella – one of life's good ones. Sure enough, an hour or so later there was a knock at the door. I answered it to find him standing there.

'Your babysitter's here,' he grinned.

That evening, although I enjoyed my night out with the girls, I found myself constantly checking my watch. I felt uneasy, but I couldn't explain why. I was also conscious not to take advantage of Adam's kind nature. When I arrived home a few hours later, I was shocked to find all the lights in my flat turned off.

'Only me,' I called out, flicking on the switch.

I half-expected to find Adam asleep on the sofa. But there was no sign of him, and weirdly, there was no sofa.

'Adam?' I called out. A knot of anxiety twisted in the pit of my stomach – something wasn't right.

I went over to the corner where my girls slept, but they weren't there. No children, and no Adam. That's when I took in the room for the first time and realised it'd been cleared out. Everything had been taken, including my children.

'Catherine… Rabiya!'

Panic overwhelmed me as I ran around the empty room, searching for a clue. Searching for anything.

I knew instantly that this wasn't anything to do with Adam, but where was he? More worryingly, where were my girls? Something was seriously wrong. For some inexplicable reason I began to open cupboards and drawers. I'd hoped to find a note explaining everything. But there was no note, and even the cupboards had been cleared. Everything had been taken, as though it was an empty flat waiting to be let out to tenants. I sat on the bare floor and put my head in my hands.

*Think,* I told myself. *Think. Where would they be? Maybe something had happened to one of the girls? Maybe he'd taken them to hospital?*

Although I'd felt tipsy when I'd first come in, panic had lifted the fog in my brain. Reality began to sink in: my girls had gone. The thought hit me as a searing pain slicing through the centre of my heart.

Mo flashed through my mind.

*Could he be behind this?* I shook the thought from my head. *No, I'd not seen him for months. He wasn't even in the country.*

I thought of Adam and shook my head once more.

*Adam loved my girls. He wouldn't do anything to harm them.*

I wanted to call the police, but something stopped me. I had a deep mistrust of them since my false arrest and imprisonment.

*No,* I thought, *there has to be a reasonable explanation.*

I felt my heart thudding violently inside my chest as panic coursed through my veins.

*My babies had been taken.*

I ran over to the sink and vomited violently. My head began to spin until I couldn't think straight. I paced up and down the room like a caged animal.

*Think, think.*

*Maybe it's got something to do with Andrea? Maybe one baby wasn't enough for her so she had to come back and get mine? Maybe Marion had called round?* I shook the thoughts from my head. *No, not in the middle of the night.*

*Maybe one of my friends had called by. But where were my children?* Nothing made sense.

I was just about to go and knock on Tariq's door when I heard someone knock on mine. I opened it up to find Adam standing there, looking distraught.

'Where are they? Where are my girls?' I roared. I grabbed him by his lapels and pushed him backwards.

Adam reeled away from me. 'I tried to stop them, Mary. I tried everything. I managed to hide Catherine, but she moved and they heard so they took her as well.'

I shook my head in confusion. He wasn't making any sense.

'Where are they, and who took them? Tell me. Tell me!' I screamed.

But Adam could barely look at me as though he didn't know how to break the news.

'Just tell me! Tell me who took my kids! It was Andrea, wasn't it?'

Adam shook his head. 'No,' he said. 'It was social services.'

I felt my legs give way as my shoulder caught and then slumped against the side of the wall. Adam took a step forward and managed to catch me before I collapsed in a heap.

'Social services?' I gasped. 'But why? Why would they take my children?'

He helped me to my feet and led me back into the room.

'I don't know, Mary. But someone rang them. When they called round they found me babysitting, that's when they took them. I tried to stop them, I really did, but they'd already got Rabiya. I tried to hide Catherine, and I did, but then they heard her.'

I waited until dawn, counting down the hours until I could ring social services. When I finally did, a social worker told me that someone had called the NSPCC and reported me.

'But who?' I demanded to know. 'I care for my girls. Who would report me?'

But she refused to say. Instead, she told where my girls could be found.

'Your children will be held at the children's home, but you are welcome to come and visit them.'

I put down the receiver and sobbed my heart out. I'd come so far, I'd fought so hard to keep my girls, but now they'd been taken and I didn't even know why.

My answer came an hour or so later when my home phone rang.

'We did good, didn't we?' A female voice cackled over the telephone. 'You should be thanking us, really.'

I didn't recognise the voice, but I knew that whoever this woman was she knew something about my children.

'What do you mean? Who is this?'

'I mean, we got rid of that nigger child of yours,' she hissed.

Rage boiled up inside me.

'Who is this?' I screamed down the line. 'Who are you, and why have you done this to me and my family?'

'I'm John's sister, and I've done you a favour.'

Suddenly, everything clicked into place. John's family had alerted the NSPCC in revenge for me calling the military police after he'd beaten me black and blue. I couldn't prove it, but I was certain they'd cleared my flat too, once they knew it was empty. I realised in that moment it'd be a long fight not only to clear my name but to get my babies back.

Catherine was just three, and Rabiya only ten months old. It simply broke my heart to see my babies inside a children's home. It was as though all the fight had been taken from me in that single moment. I felt utterly defeated. In spite of my best efforts, I'd still lost my children. The social worker had said I was allowed to visit them as often as I wanted, but that didn't stop the guilt I felt inside because I knew I'd failed them.

*I should've been there. I should've been there to protect them.* I cursed again and again. *If only I hadn't gone out that night. If only I'd have stayed at home.*

But it was no good, because I knew John, and I knew how vicious and spiteful he could be. If it hadn't been that night, it would've been another. He had obviously been watching me, waiting for me to go out, and I'd played straight into his hands.

Although they were kept at the children's home, the matron there was a kind and considerate lady who allowed me to take my girls out. However, a few weeks later, I arrived as normal only to find Rabiya missing.

'She's with a foster family,' the matron explained in a business-like voice. 'One of the care assistants took a shine to your daughter and took her home to her parents. She'll be kept in foster care for the time being.'

I started to cry; I was simply devastated.

'But they can't do that,' I wailed. 'I want her back!'

'I'm afraid they already have. But you have Catherine, so all is not lost.'

But it already was because Rabiya had been fostered out, so I knew it'd be hard to get her back. I'd saved her life, only for her to be stolen from me. Over the days and weeks that followed, I was utterly bereft. But there was nothing I could do. Back then, women who left their children with unrelated male babysitters were viewed with suspicion and wrongly judged. I'd left my girls with a male friend, so by rights, I'd already been labelled a 'bad mother'.

'How do I get my children back?' I asked the social worker one day. I was desperate because I realised the longer Rabiya was with her foster family, the less chance I had of getting her home.

'Try to get yourself a house, and then we can look at you having your children back with you. Go down to the corporation (council) offices and tell them you need a house.'

I did as she said, but the council couldn't help me.

'Unless your children are with you then you're not a priority,' a stern-faced lady behind a desk informed me. She looked over my shoulder and beckoned the next person forward.

'But social services told me to come here and get a house so I could get my children back.'

The lady seemed unmoved as though it really wasn't her problem.

'No children, no house,' she said as she moved on to help the next poor soul.

I was exasperated. It was a chicken and egg situation with no way out.

With both girls in care, I decided I'd had enough and temporarily went off the rails a bit. Everyone had already labelled me 'a bad mother', so I reasoned I may as well start acting like one. Deep down, I felt I had nothing to live for. With my children gone I had nothing left. I knew there was no point in trying for another child because it would only be taken from me. Instead, I started to drink and stay out all night. Looking back, I was out of my head with grief for my children but I didn't want to think, so I drank to forget.

I met a radio operator on board one of the ships, and his name was Stan. Stan was kind and he lavished me with gifts. He also fell in love with me, but I'd been numbed by life and alcohol and was incapable of love. So, when his ship finally set sail, and Stan got down on one knee and proposed, I accepted. I knew I didn't love him in the same way he loved me, but the drink had blunted my emotions, and I did what I had to do to survive. Stan was wealthy, and now that we were engaged, he insisted on paying money into my bank account each month so that I could buy nice things. But I didn't care about money, as long as I had enough in my purse to buy the next bottle of booze. I continued to party with friends and some other sailors they knew down on the docks. I craved affection and I didn't care where I found it. One night I spent the entire evening with another sailor. So, a few weeks later, when I began to feel nauseous I realised to my horror that I was pregnant again.

'What are you going to do?' a friend asked after I'd confided in her what had happened.

By now, my heart had hardened so much that it felt as solid as stone.

'What's the point in me bringing another child into the world? They've taken my children, and when they find out about this one, they'll take it as well. I just can't do it. I can't go through with it.'

Despite everything I'd done to keep Rabiya, I decided this time the best thing to do would be to have a termination. It went against my beliefs, but I just couldn't see another way out. I was certain that if the nuns didn't get to my child first, then social services would.

What was the point in bringing a baby into the world only to hand it over to a stranger?

'I can't do it. I'm going to have an abortion,' I decided.

I was over four months pregnant when I walked into the hospital in Edinburgh. But this time I knew I wouldn't run away. This time I'd go through with it, even if my heart was breaking inside. I told the doctor I was sure I couldn't have the baby.

'Both my children have been taken from me, and so will this one. What's the point? What sort of life will this child have?'

The doctor shook his head. It was clear to me that he must have seen this before, but it didn't make it any easier for him or for me. I was admitted to hospital and given various tablets the day before the abortion.

'You will have the procedure tomorrow, Mary. Do you understand?' the doctor asked.

I nodded. I understood, all right, but it didn't make it right.

The following morning, I was wheeled down to theatre, where two doctors were waiting to inject a long fine needle into my pregnant belly. As the needle pierced my skin I began to panic and then to struggle.

'No, no, don't!' I gasped. 'I-I-I've changed my mind.'

But it was too late. The needle had already gone inside, killing the unborn baby within my womb. The injection triggered labour pains, and I was forced to give birth to my dead child. Tears filled my eyes as I pushed my baby out into the world. I cried for the life I'd lost, and I carried on weeping until I had no tears left. When I discovered my child had been a boy, I wept more. He had been perfect in every way, just still and dead. I'd taken his life, and I would never forgive myself for what I'd done.

Afterwards, I was a mess, both physically and mentally. I hated myself, so much so that I could barely stand to look at my own reflection in the mirror.

*What have you become?* I asked myself. But I had no answers. I barely knew my own mind any more.

Friends were worried the abortion would send me further into a spiral of depression. I was, too. But just as I'd reached rock bottom something kicked in, bringing me back. I don't know if it was self-preservation, but the anger I felt at the injustice of having my children taken seemed to spur me on. With a new fighting spirit, when the matron told me that I could take Catherine out for the weekend, I decided to run. I ran to the only place I knew: I took my daughter and fled back home to Ireland.

# CHAPTER 15

## Going Home

Arriving back in Ballina, I headed straight over to Mrs Campbell's house with Catherine. My old neighbour was a little surprised but delighted to see us.

'Oh my, look how much Catherine has grown!' she exclaimed as soon as we walked in through her back door.

'I'm sorry to land ourselves on you again...' I began.

Mrs Campbell was as gracious as ever and held her hand up as though no apology was needed.

'Take your coat off and sit down. I've just made a pot of tea.'

We talked long into the afternoon, and although I didn't tell her everything, she had a rough idea of what I'd been through.

'So do you think you'll get your other child back?' she asked, taking a sip from her steaming cup of tea.

'I hope so. I'm determined no one will take my children off me again.'

The Campbells made up a bed for me. The following day, determined to make a fresh start, I headed back over to the plastics factory to ask for my old job back. Mrs Campbell looked after Catherine while I worked around the clock, trying to raise some much-needed cash for us. But word travelled fast. I'd only been back home for less than a week when there was a knock at the door. It was Friday evening and I'd just finished work. Mrs Campbell opened it and my heart sank when I saw Sister Seraphina standing there with Mrs Elroy, the social worker who'd put me in Castlepollard. Mrs Campbell's face dropped as the two women marched into her house without invitation and straight over to me.

'Are you back now, Mary?' Sister asked.

I turned away from her and lit a cigarette. My hands had begun to tremble, and I needed the cigarette to calm my nerves. Although I was older, I was wary of them and the power they seemed to hold. Mrs Elroy, the social worker, suddenly stepped forward.

'Put that cigarette out!' she demanded, scolding me as though I was still a child.

Although I felt intimidated by their presence, I didn't want them to know that. I was sick of being told what to do. I was a mother now – a working woman – not a terrified child.

'No,' I replied, blowing smoke into her face.

'Mary Creighton, you do as I tell you, or I'll have you put away.'

I looked at her and gasped. Surely she wasn't being serious? I was 20 years old, for feck's sake!

'No.'

She lifted her hand and began to poke me hard in the chest with her bony finger. 'You put that out now, or you'll never see daylight again.'

Inside, I was still trembling with fear, but the cigarette had calmed my shaking hands. 'You will not take my child off me. You will not take Catherine.'

Mrs Campbell had followed us into the kitchen and tried her best to diffuse the situation. By now, the rage I'd been holding in was about to erupt. I wanted to kill her. I wanted to kill them both for what they'd put me and Catherine through. They'd ruined my life. I'd already lost one child, and I was sure as hell that I wouldn't lose another. Opening up the back door, I marched out into the garden to search for the biggest rock I could find.

'Mary, what are you doing?'

It was Mr Campbell. He'd followed me outside.

'I want to kill her,' I screamed. 'I want to kill them both, and I will!'

I was blind with rage. I'd never known such white-hot burning anger. Lifting a rock, I held it aloft and looked towards the back of the house. I felt Mr Campbell grab my forearm with his hand and force it downwards.

'No, child,' he whispered. 'Not like this.'

It took a while, but somehow he managed not only to calm me down but also to coax me back inside the house. Both women were still there, but now Sister had decided to change tack.

'I can see you're upset, child, and you've every right to be.'

An uneasy feeling ran through me. Why was she being nice to me when she was as much to blame as the social worker? They'd been in it together from the start. I never normally swore, but by now, I didn't care.

'You can both feck off!' I bellowed.

I felt the veins on my forehead bulge with anger. Blood pulsed inside my brain, flooding my body with adrenalin, placing me on high alert.

*Don't trust them. Don't trust anything they tell you,* the voice inside my head urged.

We'd reached stalemate, so Mrs Campbell ushered them out of her house with the promise that she'd try and talk to me. But there was nothing she or anyone else could say to make me change my mind. I knew what they were here for, and this time no one was going to take my child. No one.

A week later, I came home from work to find the best china cups and saucers on the kitchen table.

My face was ashen as I turned to Mrs Campbell. 'They've been here, haven't they?'

She put down the dishcloth and turned around from the sink. 'Yes, but it's good news, Mary. Catherine is yours. The social worker isn't going to be on your back any more. It's over.'

The anxious breath I'd been holding inside came rushing out of my lungs as a huge breath of relief.

'Are you sure?'

The old lady smiled and nodded. 'Yes, she came here herself to tell me the good news. She can see that Catherine is well cared for and what a good job you're doing. It's over, child. You can keep Catherine.'

I could barely believe it. At last, things were finally looking up for me. With my eldest child now safe, and money in the bank, I embarked on the second part of my plan: to bring Rabiya back home. I travelled over to Edinburgh and asked Marion if she could look after Catherine for me.

'I've just got to deal with a bit of business,' I said. 'I'll see you later.'

I'd planned to go to the children's home the following morning. That night, some friends invited me out for a drink. I'd not been around, so I was desperate to catch up with them. It was the end of summer, and a particularly warm evening, so I decided to walk back home alone. I was just thinking of the future and how happy we would be – me and my two girls together – when I felt someone grab me from behind. We struggled. They put one hand against my neck and covered my mouth with the other hand to stop me from screaming out. I tried to claw away both hands, but then I felt a heavy blow to the back of my head. I looked upwards towards the sky, but suddenly everything blurred and I collapsed against the street below. Everything went black, and then there was nothing.

The following day, I awoke in a hospital bed. I felt groggy and confused, unable to piece together my surroundings.

'W-w-what happened?' I asked a passing nurse. 'Where am I?'

I ached all over. I lifted the sheet and peered down – I'd been beaten black and blue. Even my hands were covered in deep purple bruises.

'You were mugged,' the nurse said, coming over to check me over. She took out a thermometer and placed it in my mouth. 'You need to rest. Someone found you on the street, you see. The police think you may have been robbed, because you had nothing on you when they brought you in. We didn't know who you were.'

Over the days that followed, I told the nurses who I was and that I needed to get out to see my daughters, but they insisted on keeping me in for observation. I remained inside the hospital for four days, from Sunday to Wednesday. As soon as I was discharged, I went straight to Marion's house, but Catherine had gone.

'I didn't know where you were,' Marion said, her arms folded across her pinched little chest. 'So I called social services. They came and took her away.'

My mouth fell open and I staggered backwards as though she'd just punched me.

'But I was in hospital! I was mugged!'

The bruises were still evident on my face, neck, and hands where I'd tried to fight off my attacker, but Marion seemed unconvinced.

'But you've looked after Catherine before. You know I always come back for her.'

I watched as Marion shifted uneasily. A flicker of guilt passed over her face, and that's when I knew it – something had happened.

'What? What is it?'

Marion refused to make eye contact, and instead talked downwards towards the ground.

'It was Anne,' she began. 'Your Aunt Anne was in Scotland, visiting relatives, so she popped in to see me. Catherine was here, so she asked where you were. That's when I told her, I didn't know.'

I listened intently, but I was still confused.

'But what has Aunt Anne got to do with this?'

Marion lifted her head and looked over at me for the first time.

'Well, that's it. She said she was taking Catherine back to America with her. Helen was here, so we told her no. But then she said something... Oh, Mary, I'm sorry... but Sister Seraphina had promised Catherine to her all along. Anne even said it. She turned to us and said, "That child was supposed to be mine."'

I was stunned. There'd been a plan, and one of my father's sisters had been at the root of it. She'd been in cahoots with Sister Seraphina all along. She'd bought me slippers as a child and then tried to steal my child from me.

I could tell by the look on Marion's face that there was more. 'Go on,' I urged.

I watched as she twisted her hands in her lap anxiously.

'I was frightened. Frightened that Anne would come back and steal Catherine, so that's why I called social services. I asked them to come and get her, so they took her back to the children's home.'

I gasped.

'But she's my child!'

'Yes,' Marion hissed. 'But I didn't know where you'd gone.'

Exasperated, I marched straight over to the children's home, where I demanded to see Matron.

'I'm sorry, Mary, but you can't take her over the threshold, not after what happened last time.'

'But she's my daughter!'

Matron shook her head but then she began to soften slightly. 'You can try and fight for Catherine, but you'll never get Rabiya back. It's her foster family, you see. They'll never give her up, not now.'

'Well, I'll go round there and get her myself.'

I felt her hand on my shoulder as she tried to stop me.

'They've moved, Mary. They moved a while ago, and I'm not allowed to tell you where they are.'

I looked at her in astonishment.

'But you can still see Catherine, although you're only allowed to take her to the door, not through it.'

As soon as I saw Catherine, I felt as though my heart had been ripped in two. In spite of everything, my fresh start and the new life I thought I'd built for my girls, I'd somehow managed to lose everything. I'd lost my babies all over again.

That evening I left Catherine behind in the children's home and went straight to the nearest off-licence to buy myself a bottle of whiskey. In the days and weeks that followed, I bought vodka, cognac, or anything else I could lay my hands on. I used alcohol to blot out my pain, to try and numb myself against life and reality. I used it as an anaesthetic against the very real fear that I'd never get my children back again.

# CHAPTER 16

# Going Off the Rails

In a haze of drink and hangovers, I lurched from one day to the next, not knowing what to do or where life would dump me. I fell into a deep spiral of depression and allowed it to drag me so low that I was hardly able to look after myself, never mind someone else. I had nothing left to lose because I'd already had the two most important things taken from me. With my life going nowhere, I decided to hitchhike with a group of friends to Birkenhead, where I met a girl called Jean. She and I would go down to the docks and date sailors, who would lavish us with fancy meals out. In truth I just craved love, and although it wasn't the right kind, this love felt better than no love at all. Following my abusive relationship with Mo and my tough upbringing in Ireland, I convinced myself it was all I deserved.

'Come and stay at mine, if you like?' Jean suggested, so I took her up on her offer.

Jean lived with her mother, a lovely lady called Maria. Although I was a stranger, as soon as I walked in through her front door, I was welcomed with open arms and Maria treated me as though I was her own flesh and blood. I was surrounded by love, but the fog of depression refused to lift. I'd lost contact with my girls and I despised myself for it. I felt a failure both as a mother and a human being.

One day, in the pit of despair, I got down on my hands and knees and frantically searched the bathroom cabinet. I don't remember what pills I swallowed but I hoped I'd taken enough to dull the deep sense of loss and guilt I lived with every day. Maria found me and called an ambulance, not that I can recall any of it. She was a good person, so when I was discharged from hospital and turned up on her doorstep again she didn't turn me away or ask questions.

'I just want you to be all right, Mary,' she said, enveloping me in her arms.

My body fell against her as I sobbed. But, try as I might, I couldn't find the words to explain why I'd tried to end my own life. I knew why, but trying to articulate the deep sense of loss of losing both children had seemed impossible. A few months later, I did it again. Without my girls there seemed no point in going on. This time, the doctors decided it would be best if I was admitted to a psychiatric hospital for my own safety. I remained in the hospital as an inpatient for six weeks. That was, until another girl stole a pair of red shoes and hid one under my bed. A search was organised, but when a staff member found it underneath my mattress I was summoned to see the psychiatrist. First, I sat down on my bed and put all my belongings in a bag. Then I walked calmly into his office.

He eyed me with suspicion as I walked in through the door.

'Ah,' he said, spotting the bag in my hands, 'I see you've already packed.'

'Yes.'

'Good, because we can't have thieves in here, so you must leave today because—'

But I didn't want to listen to any more. Before he'd even finished his sentence, I'd left the room and walked out of the hospital for ever. With nowhere else to go, I returned to Maria's house, where I stayed for another nine or ten months. Towards the end of summer 1973, I woke up early one morning and had a moment of complete clarity.

*I don't want to drink any more. The drink is depressing me, it's ruining my life.*

With a renewed sense of purpose, I decided to return home to Ireland and to Ballina. Thankfully, I managed to get my old job back, working in the plastics factory. I'd kept in touch with Stan, who had continued to put money into my bank account so that I didn't have to worry. Over the past year or so, the money had built up so much that I didn't have to work, but I chose to. I had to keep myself busy and keep off the bottle if I was going to survive.

Mrs Campbell stepped in and offered to let me live with her, but I felt I'd already brought enough trouble to her door, so I stayed with an old friend who lived opposite the Campbells, called Brenda.

I'd been back in Ireland for four or five months when a fella I'd known since we'd both been 11 years old asked me out. I was extremely flattered because Niall was a lovely lad, and quite a catch. Not only was he good-looking, he also had Irish charm by the bucket-load. One date led to another, and soon I found myself falling for him. At 27, Niall was five years older than me, but in many ways I felt older because I'd had the worst things in life thrown at me. We'd been dating for a while when one thing led to another and we ended up in bed together. For the first time in my life I felt I'd found someone who loved me for the girl I was. As I lay next to him in bed, I absorbed all the contours of his beautiful face. I'd never known happiness like it.

'So, when are we going to see each other again?' I asked.

I ran my fingers through his hair and kissed him tenderly on the lips. I'd fallen for Niall, and there seemed no point in wasting any more time.

'Erm, I'm not sure,' he said, leaping up and pulling his underwear back on.

I sat bolt upright in bed. 'What do you mean?'

Niall turned to me. I watched as his fingers worked quickly, buttoning up his shirt as fast as he could. Then he reached for his trousers off the side.

'Well, you see, Mary, it's difficult. It's, erm, well, it's just that I'm, erm… married.'

My face dropped. I'd hoped Niall was different but he was as bad as the rest. I grabbed a pillow and threw it as hard as I could at his head.

'Oww! What was that for?'

All the love I'd felt for him had gone flying out of the window. Now all I wanted to do was kill him!

'You'll pay for this, Niall, let me tell you!'

It had been a pathetic response – a weak threat, but I felt well and truly heartbroken. Not that he cared how I felt because he'd already bolted for it, picking up his shoes as he ran out of the door.

Afterwards, I felt devastated because I'd stupidly believed Niall had loved me as much as I'd loved him. So, a month or so later when the familiar sickness descended I didn't need a test or a trip to the doctor's to tell me that I was pregnant. I was beside myself with worry. I knew Niall wouldn't have anything to do with me – I was on my own, and not for the first time. I thought about travelling to Liverpool on the ferry, but I wasn't sure where I'd go.

Maybe I could go to Maria's house, or maybe one of my friends would help me out?

All these ideas and more swirled about inside my head, making me feel dizzy. The only thing I was certain of right now was that I wouldn't return to Scotland, because if I did, social services were sure to take away my child. I also knew I'd never be able to have another abortion. I'd had one and it had almost broken me in two. The only thing I was certain of right now was that I couldn't take another life. I didn't want to ask the Campbells for help again because they'd already done so much for me. Besides, I couldn't bear to see the disappointment on their faces. In a daze I found myself walking almost robotically towards my old school, and as I knocked on the door, it was Sister Celestine who answered. She had once been my old teacher and I trusted her more than Sister Seraphina. And right now I had to trust someone. I just needed someone to talk to, and I knew that Sister Celestine would listen and hopefully give me some good advice on what to do.

'Yes, child?' Sister answered.

'I-I-I...' I stammered, as I stood there unable to get the words out.

Sister realised something was seriously wrong and ushered me into a side room, where she told me to sit down. I watched as she walked over to the door and closed it.

'Oh, Sister,' I said, beginning to break down, 'I came here because I didn't have anywhere else to go.'

'Mary, my child, there's nothing you can say that will shock me, and there's nothing that cannot be sorted. I am here to listen, and I am here to help you.'

Now she'd given me permission, suddenly the flood-gates opened as the whole sorry tale came spilling out. As it came tumbling out of my mouth, I trusted that everything I told her in that small room would be confidential.

'And now I'm pregnant,' I wept. 'But the father, well, he's married, so he doesn't want anything to do with me…'

Sister's face was full of sympathy as she leaned forward in her chair and gently took my hand in hers, patting it lightly.

'…and I can't return to Scotland, because I'm scared they'll take my child. They've already taken my daughters from me. Oh, Sister,' I said, gasping for breath, 'what am I going to do?'

She let go of my hand and rose to her feet.

'Leave it with me, child, I'll help you.'

'Will you?' I asked, looking up at her with tear-stained eyes.

'Of course I will.'

With that she left the room. Although I had confided in her, it turned out that Sister Celestine was as bad as all the others. As soon as she'd left me, she walked down the hallway and into the main office to use the telephone. With the door closed, Sister picked up the receiver and dialled a number. As I sat there weeping, unbeknownst to me, she had spoken to a woman to 'make arrangements'. That woman had been Mrs Elroy, the social worker who had already ruined my life. Between them, Sister and Mrs Elroy cooked up a plan. It was so wicked, my life at Castlepollard would feel like a walk in the park compared to where I was about to be sent.

# CHAPTER 17

## The Magdalene Laundry

A day or so after I'd confided in her, Sister Celestine turned up at the Campbells' back door wanting to speak with me. Standing behind her was Mrs Elroy, the social worker.

'Can we come in?' Sister asked Terry Campbell as he answered the door.

However, after what had happened before, Terry was suspicious. 'What for?'

'It's Mary, she's expecting us.'

Mr Campbell led both women through into the kitchen, where I was sitting.

'Hello, Mary,' Sister said breezily.

The arrival of the social worker had taken me by surprise, and for a moment the shock had rendered me speechless. As far as I was concerned I'd only told Sister, I hadn't expected her to involve Mrs Elroy. I realised then that she was as bad as all the other nuns who had betrayed me. They were all in this together.

'W-w-what's she doing here?' I asked, pointing directly to her.

'Now, now, Mary, don't you be getting yourself upset. Mrs Elroy is here to help you.'

But Mr Campbell wasn't convinced. He looked over at his wife, but she shrugged. Neither of them had a clue what this was about because I'd only told Sister.

'What's going on, Mary?' Terry asked, turning to me.

I felt myself flush crimson with embarrassment as I began to explain to them that I was pregnant again. I felt as though I'd let them both down. After all, it'd only been down to them that I'd managed to escape Castlepollard.

'I'm sorry,' I apologised. My voice trailed away as they both stood there trying to absorb the news.

There was a pause before Mrs Campbell came over and wrapped a kind arm around my shoulder.

'Now then, Mary. You have nothing to be sorry for,' she insisted, holding me close. Then she turned towards the two women. 'But why are you here?'

'We're here to help Mary,' Mrs Elroy replied.

I shot her a hateful look.

'What? Like last time?' I sneered like a petulant teenager.

Mrs Elroy turned to me. 'I'm not putting you in Castlepollard, if that's what you mean. I'll put you in a better place.'

My gut instinct told me not to trust her, but Sister Celestine assured me she was telling the truth.

'You won't be going back to that place, Mary, I can promise you that. We're sending you to a lovely home in

Dunboyne in Meath. It's near Dublin, and it's a beautiful place to have your baby.'

I still felt uneasy, but I'd backed myself into a corner and I didn't know how to fight my way out.

If I didn't go with them, how would I manage? Would they just take my child off me anyway?

Surely, at least if I did as they said then I'd stand a fighting chance of bringing my child home?

I wasn't keen because I didn't trust the social worker at all. But following a long discussion, I realised that I didn't have much choice now that she knew I was pregnant. If I didn't agree to go along with them, they'd find me and take my baby from me anyway. Despite a lot of apprehension on my part, I reluctantly agreed to go along with their plan.

'Good, that's all decided then,' Sister said with a satisfied smile. I noticed her eyes shoot sideward towards the social worker. Mrs Elroy returned a look that left me feeling uneasy. But both women were adamant I'd go to Dunboyne Castle and everything would be fine.

'You must trust us, Mary. We are trying to help you,' Sister added as she got up and left.

Three days later, a driver arrived in a huge black car to drive me the 140 miles to Dunboyne Castle. It was a private hospital taxi and inside sat Sister and Mrs Elroy.

'Good morning, Mary,' Sister grinned. She patted a seat and urged me to climb in the back of the car next to her. 'Isn't it a beautiful day?'

But I didn't answer because I couldn't. I felt like a bundle of nerves. I was doing the very thing I promised myself I'd never do – trust the nuns again.

We travelled along country roads for almost three hours, stopping off for a bite to eat halfway there. As we drove along, I looked out of the window to try and see where we were. I spotted a couple of signs for Dublin and breathed a sigh of relief: we were going exactly where they said we would. They'd been telling the truth. As the countryside whizzed by in a blur, I settled back in my seat.

Everything's going to be all right, I told myself.

Soon afterwards, we passed two pillars at the side of the road and the driver signalled right. As we pulled into the grounds, I craned my neck to see what Dunboyne Castle looked like. But instead of beautiful rolling grounds as I'd imagined, I was greeted with a large, old-fashioned convent and another building with a cross on top of the roof. The car pulled to a halt outside the main entrance. The large wooden door swung open as a middle-aged nun stepped out into the driveway to greet us. The nun was dressed head-to-toe in black, and she was so hard-faced that I convinced myself she was actually a man in drag.

'Sister,' she said, nodding towards Sister Celestine as though they were already familiar with one another.

Sister and Mrs Elroy walked over to speak with her, leaving me in the car. Shortly afterwards, Mrs Elroy came over towards me.

'You're staying here tonight, Mary. The driver is tired, so you need to come inside,' she said, helping me out of the car.

I felt uneasy. I'd never trusted her, and I didn't trust her now.

'But I thought I was going to Dunboyne Castle?'

The social worker sighed as though she didn't have time for this.

'Mary, I've just told you. The driver is tired and needs to rest, so you will be staying here. It'll only be for one night.'

I stopped and looked her directly in the eye.

'And I can leave in the morning to go to Dunboyne Castle?'

Mrs Elroy held my gaze.

'Yes.'

My instinct told me something was wrong, and I couldn't shake off an uneasy feeling rising from the pit of my stomach. But we were here now, and it was only for one night. That's what she'd said, so I put my trust in the hands of the two women.

'All right, I suppose I'll have to.'

The older nun led us all inside and we were shown into a room. Once again, the women spoke in a corner of the room in hushed voices as I waited to be told where I'd be resting for the night. Then I saw Sister gesture over to the other nun and, without a word or a second glance, Sister Celestine and Mrs Elroy left. They'd only been inside the room a matter of minutes.

'Where am I?' I asked the older nun after they'd left.

The bad feeling I'd had before had come back with a vengeance.

'You're in Dublin,' the nun replied.

'But I'm supposed to be going to County Meath.'

I waited for a reply, but she said nothing. Instead she beckoned me to follow her along the corridor and up some stairs to the first floor. From there I was taken into a large square room with half a dozen beds lined up inside it.

'That one is yours,' the nun said, pointing one out to me.

The room had felt gloomy to say the least, but I reasoned it'd only be for one night. The door leading into it was wooden but arched-shaped at the top, like a church door. There was one window but it was high up in the eaves and so let in very little light. In fact, it was so high that you'd have to stand on a bed just to try and look outside. There were lockers beside each of the seven beds, one sink, a wardrobe, and a couple of mirrors. There was also a door that led off the room and through into a toilet. Even with shoes on, the bare floorboards looked as though they'd be cold underfoot. My eyes scoured the room for other clues. I noticed that the top half of the wall had been painted virgin blue but the bottom half was brown. There was a speaker perched up on the wall just below the high window. But there was something about the layout of the room that had set my senses on high alert.

'T-t-this isn't another mother-and-baby home, is it?' I asked, turning to face the nun, but when I looked around she'd vanished.

I'd no sooner put my things in the locker than it was time for bed. As soon as other women began to enter the room I breathed a sigh of relief. It couldn't be a mother-and-baby unit because the women were far too old. Also, unlike me, none of them were pregnant. The youngest woman after me was in her forties. But the others were mainly in their fifties and sixties, with a few in their seventies. Altogether the home held 40 or so women, with seven in my dormitory. Although it was clear that I was the only pregnant woman there, I was treated no differently to the others. Sure enough, as soon as we were in our beds, the nun turned out the light and locked the door, sealing us inside the dorm for the rest of the evening. I didn't talk to the other women because I didn't know what to say. They were all so much older than me, and their eyes seemed vacant, as though they'd been institutionalised. I recognised that same stare in the eyes of some of the girls at Castlepollard. It was a stare that said, I'm resigned to my fate, and this is my life from now on. A shudder ran through me as I fell into a fitful night's sleep. I hoped and prayed I'd never become like that.

The following morning we were awoken by the sound of prayer that blared through the tannoy above our heads. I watched as each woman climbed out of her bed and began to dress robotically as though she'd been drugged.

Thank goodness I'm getting out of here today, I thought as I followed them and began to pull on my own clothes. I could hardly wait. I was so eager that, by the time the nun had unlocked the door, I was ready and waiting.

'I'm leaving today,' I told her. 'They're taking me to Dunboyne Castle.'

But she didn't answer. Instead, she had a question for me.

'Do you have a middle name?'

'Yes, it's Catherine.'

'Good, that will be your name from now on.'

I was gripped with panic.

'But I'm not staying, I'm leaving here. They're picking me up. I'm having a baby, you see.' I placed a hand on my pregnant stomach as the nun looked down in disdain. 'I'm not staying here, so you don't have to change my name, I—'

She held up her hand either to shush or strike me, I couldn't be sure which. I automatically flinched.

'No, you're going to work,' she insisted, as though the matter wasn't up for discussion.

My heart thudded hard inside my chest as the palms of my hands began to sweat. I balled them for courage and then spoke again.

'No, no, you've made a mistake. I'm not meant to be here. It was the driver, you see. He was tired. They dropped me off so he could rest. I'm travelling to Dunboyne Castle today. Sister Celestine, you need to speak to her – she's the one who's arranged it.'

But nun had already turned away. 'You are here to work, and you will do so.'

With that she marched off along the corridor away from me. I was screaming inside because my gut instinct had been right all along: I'd been tricked.

I was numb as I was led through to a huge laundry room, where I was shown by one of the older women how to tag laundry. After four days, and despite my constant protests, I realised the black car was never coming back for me. I'd been tricked by two women – a nun and a social worker – and now I found myself pregnant and abandoned in High Park – Ireland's largest Magdalene Laundry. That night I cried myself to sleep.

How could I have been so gullible? I cursed as I beat my fists against my pillow. Like Castlepollard before, I'd been trapped once more, only judging by the age of the women I couldn't imagine when or how I'd get out or see daylight again. Instead, my life became one never-ending routine of drudgery. Once I'd got the hang of tagging clothes, I was moved, this time to pressing doctors' coats on a large pressing machine.

'I'm not meant to be here. I'm meant to be going to a place called Dunboyne,' I told a woman who was working next to me.

I didn't know her name, but then again, she didn't offer it or even introduce herself.

'I'm waiting for my brother,' she said in a monotone. 'He's coming to pick me up.'

Steam rose from the machine and evaporated against my skin. 'Is he?'

She nodded. 'Yes. He'll be here today, I know he will.'

Later that afternoon, I spoke to one of the other women working in the laundry.

'I'm not meant to be in here. I'm getting picked up, like that woman over there,' I said, pointing over to the large-bosomed lady I'd been speaking to earlier.

'Which one? Which woman?'

I pointed over towards the dark-haired lady on the other side of the room.

'Mary-Colette?' my new colleague asked me.

'I don't know her name.'

'What did she say?' she asked, folding some freshly ironed clothes into a pile.

'She said she's waiting for her brother. She said he's coming to pick her up.'

The older woman shrugged as though she didn't believe a word of it.

'Why? Isn't he coming?' I asked.

She sighed and put the iron down on the ironing board, perching it on its end so that it didn't scald her.

'Mary-Colette has been here since she was a child. She's been waiting for her brother to pick her up for the past 30 years.'

I gasped. 'And he never has? The brother, I mean.'

The woman shook her head, picked up her iron, and went back to her work.

'They never do,' she muttered.

Steam billowed high into the air for the rest of the day, turning the laundry into a sauna. The work was hot and the days were long. To make matters worse, we weren't even allowed a drop of water to quench our thirst. The only food and drink we received was whatever was served at dinner time. Unlike Castlepollard, there was no conversation either. It was just eat, work, and pray – nothing else. It was as though the fighting spirit of all the women had been stolen. As we ate in the dining hall, a stony-faced nun sat at a top table presided over us all. There were four women to each table, but no one dare speak for fear of punishment. It became apparent over the weeks that followed that most of the women had been sent to High Park as children and were then simply forgotten. I later learned that some had been wives, suffering from post-natal depression. On the words of their husbands, they had been incarcerated inside the laundry never to see the outside world again. Their errant husbands were simply able to carry on and remarry without guilt or repercussion because their 'wives' had been labelled 'insane'.

High Park had once been an orphanage, and there was a rumour going round that one of the women, Roisin, had taken several pairs of little girls' knickers from it. I'd been warned Roisin was odd, and to stay away from her.

By nature, she was a curt and unfriendly woman, who kept herself to herself anyway, so it wasn't difficult to stay clear of her.

'She's a strange one, her,' one of the older women whispered as we toiled away in the laundry one afternoon. 'Keep your distance.'

But the following morning, I was told I had to go and help Roisin out. Her job involved working a huge mangle at the other end of the laundry. I watched as she twisted the handle with arms as big as a man. The two huge rolling pins turned together, crushing and squeezing excess water out of the wet clothes and dripping into a steel bucket below. As soon as she spotted me standing there, she grunted as though my help wasn't wanted or even needed. Wiping her brow with the back of her hand, she pointed to a wet pile of clothes and gestured for me to pass them over. As I leaned in to pick the first shirt up, Roisin bent over in front of me and began to turn the mangle to finish off the job in hand. As she did so, the hem of her grubby skirt lifted up, revealing a pair of patchwork knickers that barely covered her ample backside. I started to laugh because it was true: Roisin had stolen a ton of little girls' knickers all right, but she wasn't a pervert as the other women had suspected. Instead, she'd stitched them together to make a big pair for herself.

I started to howl with laughter, and soon I couldn't stop. Tears of mirth streamed down my face as Roisin turned to look at me with a quizzical look on her face.

I couldn't tell her why I was laughing. In fact, I couldn't tell anyone because I was doubled up in hysterics over what I'd just seen. Roisin didn't seem very impressed, and huffing and rolling her eyes skyward, she grabbed the next garment from the top of the pile and began to feed it into the mangle. For me, it was a rare moment of joy in an otherwise grim and unwelcoming world. It later transpired that Roisin's knickers weren't the only handmade thing at High Park laundry.

In the middle of the room stood a large metal bucket that contained bloodied water. When I first spotted it I presumed someone must have had an accident. The crimson water reminded me of the bucket of guts I'd seen in the bedpan back at Castlepollard. But the bucket had nothing to do with afterbirth. On closer inspection, I realised it was full of sanitary towels, made up from old rags and stitched together. The women would place their used and bloodied rags inside the 'slop' bucket, soaking them, before they were washed and handed out to be reused. The bucket of blood made me feel sick – I was just thankful that I was pregnant and so had no use for such things. Well, not for quite a few months, at least.

Each morning it'd be the same grinding routine. We'd rise at 6.30 to the sound of prayers and go straight to Mass an hour later. Breakfast would be served at eight, or 8.30, depending on how long the priest had rambled on, and then we'd work until lunch at midday. The food was terrible and, to make matters worse, it was the same food every single day. At breakfast we could choose either porridge or eggs, and for lunch and dinner it would be either a thin vegetable broth and bread, or shepherd's pie. I'd permanently be both hungry and thirsty. Working inside the laundry left us dehydrated, but there was no access to taps or water. There was one tap inside the laundry, but everyone had had their dirty work hands on it. It was also used to rinse out stinking clothes, so no one went near it or put their mouth near it, no matter how desperate they were. Instead, we all suffered in silence.

I'd been at High Park a month when I was sent to Holles Street hospital in Dublin, for a pregnancy check-up.

'You are to get the bus, Catherine,' one of the nuns instructed me, using my middle name. 'Here's some money to get there. There's not a penny less or more, and you shall return here once you are done. Do you understand?'

I nodded. Secretly, I was delighted because I was getting out, even if it was only for a few hours.

I watched as the elderly nun carefully counted out the pennies into my hand as though she'd taken them from her own purse. I had no intention of catching the bus because I still had funds of my own in the bank and I intended to use them. Once I was out of sight, I headed up the street to hail a taxi. I went to the hospital as planned, but also took a bit of time to myself to look around Dublin, because I knew the nuns would never find out. Unsurprisingly, I was in no rush to get back to work.

I'd enjoyed my day outside High Park so much that I decided to make up an imaginary appointment a week or so later.

'It's the baby,' I told one of the nuns. 'They want to check it's growing properly.'

The nun listened and then nodded in agreement.

'Very well. Wait here while I go and fetch you some money for your bus fare.'

I smiled to myself. I'd finally found a way to beat the system and escape the laundry, even if it was only for a day. I wondered if I should use the opportunity to escape. Then I remembered – I had nowhere to go. I didn't know a soul in Dublin, and if I went back to Ballina, Sister Seraphina or Sister Celestine would be sure to find me and drag me back to the laundry. I thought about catching a ferry over to England, but I was terrified that as soon as I had the baby, they'd take it from me anyway.

No, I reasoned. I'd stay at High Park until I had the baby and then I'd find a way to get us out, just as I had at Castlepollard.

'There you go, Catherine,' the nun said, counting every single penny out into the palm of my hand. 'And you come straight back, understand?'

I smiled and nodded at her. I was 22 now – I was older and wiser – and I knew how to play their game.

As soon as the door opened, I took a deep breath and walked off happily down the path and away from the laundry. Once I was out of sight, I hailed another cab and travelled into the centre of Dublin, where I spent the day shopping for baby clothes. Once purchased, I took them out of their packaging and stuffed them deep inside my rucksack so that the nuns wouldn't see them. I wandered around the whole afternoon. I was just about to head over towards Guineys, a large department store in Talbot Street, when I decided against it. My legs were aching, and Dublin was packed because the buses were on strike. There seemed to be thousands of people out shopping and I simply couldn't be bothered to battle my way through the crowds much longer. I glanced down at my watch: it was 5.30. I knew I'd be pushing my luck to stay out much longer, so I turned around and went in search of a cab. I knew if I was out too long the nuns would check with the hospital and I'd be rumbled.

No, I decided, I needed to be sensible. That way I could come out time and time again.

Waiting on the side of the road, I held out a hand to try and hail a cab. 'Taxi!'

Thankfully, even though Dublin was heaving, a few moments later, one pulled up.

'Thanks for stopping,' I said and smiled gratefully at the driver.

'Where to, young lady?' he asked.

I'd just put a foot inside the cab when there was an almighty boom. The sound was so loud that it reverberated through the ground and almost knocked me off my feet.

'What the heck was that?' I exclaimed.

'I don't know, but it didn't sound good.'

The taxi driver craned his neck out of the side widow to look behind him, but we couldn't see anything. Other folk stopped and looked around them too. The noise had been so loud that it had startled us all. We were all puzzled because no one knew what it was or where it had come from.

'It sounded like an explosion,' the cabbie said as he lifted off his handbrake and we drove back to High Park.

'Well, it must have been a big one because I felt the ground shake underneath my feet,' I replied.

I was four months pregnant, but I hadn't a clue how close I'd just come to death. A few streets away, a bomb had been detonated in a blue mink Ford Escort that had been parked opposite Guineys department store. Twelve people had been killed that day, and another two died later in hospital. Thirteen of the 14 victims had been women, including one who had been nine months pregnant. Several other people lost limbs in the attack. The explosion had been the second of four in a series of co-ordinated bombings in Dublin and Monaghan, in what would become one of the deadliest attacks of a conflict known as the Troubles. We had no access to newspapers at High Park, so it wasn't until the next morning that I learned what had happened when I overheard one of the delivery boys talking to his boss.

'They say one woman's body was found on the roof of a building,' the lad said as they unpacked the van.

The older man nodded his head grimly.

'I heard four bodies were found on the street outside Guineys. People covered them in newspaper until they could be recovered.'

The boy shuddered and put down a box on the side. 'Dunt dare thinking about, does it?'

Panic set in when I realised it'd been a terrorist attack and I'd only escaped it by sheer luck. My chest heaved as my breathing became laboured and I struggled to breathe. I felt hot, clammy, and panicked all at the same time. I was scared – terrified I was having a heart attack. But it wasn't a heart attack, it was a panic attack, and after that day I began to suffer from them regularly.

*That could've been me. I could've been like that other pregnant lady,* I thought, as the grim reality swirled around inside my head. I'd been stupid to wander the streets alone. As much as I hated High Park, at least I was safe there.

Although we worked eight-hour days, we weren't paid. In short, we were slaves – slaves to the nuns and the High Park Convent. Sunday was our only day of respite, but even then, we were forced to attend church for an hour and a half. Afterwards, we'd be led back inside a large room, where the women would all sit and stare blankly at one another. No one had anything to say because no one had done anything. Sundays were strange, because inside the room women of all ages would sit clutching handbags to their chests, waiting for a relative or friend to pick them up. Most were elderly and they'd been waiting with their handbags for decades, but no one ever came to collect them. It was heartbreaking to see. As my eyes scanned all the lonely faces, I felt a sudden and unexpected pain flood through my chest. I clutched a hand against it and gasped for air.

*What if I ended up like them?* I began to panic. *What if I gave birth to my baby and they put me back in here? What if I died in this place?*

I looked across the room of female statues and shook my head.

*No, I wouldn't let it happen. I'd escaped that bomb and it'd been a miracle, but I'd escaped it for a reason, and that was to live.*

*I'm getting out of High Park*, I vowed. *If it's the last thing I do, I'm getting out of here – I have to.*

In many ways, those Sunday afternoons were worse than working flat out because there was nothing to do. No conversation and nothing to read, only a deafening silence. Our only 'treat', if you could call it that, was an hour of television one hour a week. We'd file into a corner of the room, where a large black-and-white television had been placed. There were two or three dozen chairs all lined up to face it. Once we were seated, a nun would come in and switch the TV on so we could watch

Benny Hill. She was his biggest fan and would sit there giggling throughout. I don't know why it always had to be *The Benny Hill Show*, but I suspect it was because it was the only show she liked. Even though I didn't much care for him or his humour, I'd take the opportunity to go and watch because it was the only thing that broke up the tedious boredom of life at High Park. However, women would shift and fidget constantly in front of you, so if you were unlucky enough to be sat at the back it was impossible to see the screen anyway.

We didn't get much time, or indeed, opportunity, to wash at High Park either, because the working days were so long. We'd wake up exhausted and fall into bed equally exhausted. However, one day, I felt sweaty from working in the laundry and so I asked if I could have a bath.

'The baths are upstairs,' one of the Sisters informed me curtly. 'You may have one if you want.'

Delighted, I gathered up my things and climbed the stairs. I envisaged a long, hot soak – long enough to take away the aches and pains of the back-breaking work. But as soon as I'd opened up the door to the bathroom, the smile slipped from my face. There were four bathtubs inside and they were all utterly filthy! The top half of the room had been painted a horrible pink and the bottom half was blue coloured tongue-and-groove wooden panels that had seen better days. There were four cubicles in total with a solid wall between each. Although it'd been designed for that very purpose, it offered limited privacy. Above each bath was a rail with a plastic curtain, but they'd all been drawn, revealing just how disgusting the bath tubs were inside. Each tub was coated in a thick black scum and they looked as though they'd never been cleaned. They were so filthy that I was scared to climb in one in case my baby caught a disease.

'There's nothing else for it,' I decided, rolling up my sleeves.

I glanced around the room, trying to decide which tub was the least dirty of the lot. I settled on one, nipped back downstairs, picked up some cloths, a scrubbing brush, and a bar of carbolic soap, and I began to scrub. However, the bath was much dirtier than I'd first thought and it took me ages to remove the stubborn scum. After three hours of scrubbing, I finally felt satisfied it was clean enough to use. Turning on both taps, I began to pour myself a well-earned bath. The water felt heavenly as I dipped my body into it. My swollen belly protruded above the water line like a flesh-coloured island. I stayed there until the water had turned cold. I was just about to climb out when I felt a fleeting movement. I lay there in wonder as the mound in my belly began to move and shift with the life within. My unborn child had become real in that single moment. I clasped both hands over my stomach, feeling the twists and turns of limbs as they moved inside my womb.

I realised I was luckier than most because I'd be a mother soon. I'd bring a whole new life into the world, and I vowed to protect it at all costs. With the bathwater now cold, I climbed out, grabbed my towel, and patted myself dry. Pulling the bath plug out, I watched as the water swirled around and drained from the tub. After a quick swish out, I left the bath clean for the next woman.

Later that evening, I passed the same set of stairs that led up to the bathroom when I noticed a long and winding queue. I wondered what everyone was waiting for so I tapped one woman lightly on the shoulder.

'What's happening? Why's everyone lined up?'

She turned to me and smiled.

'Haven't you heard? Someone has cleaned one of the bathtubs out, and now everyone wants to have a bath.'

I grinned and turned away. The three hours I'd spent scrubbing would benefit everyone, not just me.


I often thought about what Mrs Elroy, the social worker, had said, back in Mrs Campbell's house. She'd threatened to put me away and she had, for the second time.

When I wasn't laundering doctors' coats from the hospitals, I'd launder denim jeans and striped denim jackets of prisoners from the local prisons. I'd never stolen a thing in my life, apart from the doctor's daffodils, but the prisoners' jeans were such good quality that I was tempted to stow a pair away for myself. There was only one thing that stopped me: the way my luck was going, I was certain to be caught and probably flung inside the prison as a suspected escapee.

No, I decided. I'd better not risk it.

We were also expected to wash hotel sheets and towels, domestic clothes and robes belonging to the priests. The laundry, it seemed, ran quite a profitable business, not that we ever saw a penny of it.

Almost six weeks after I'd been dumped at High Park, a nun came to see me.

'You have a visitor, Catherine.'

I was a little startled and wondered who it could be as I followed her along the corridor and into a side room on the ground floor. As I approached the door, I prayed it'd be Mr Campbell, and that he'd come to rescue me. But as the nun pushed it open, I saw the last person I'd expected to see sitting there.

'Sister Celestine!' I gasped.

'Hello, child,' she smiled, patting a hand against the seat next to her as though we were old friends.

'If you think I'm going to sit next to you after what you've done to me then...' I snapped as anger overwhelmed me. I clenched my fists to try and contain it.

'I didn't know, Mary,' Sister said innocently.

'Of course you knew! You cooked it up between you, you and that fecking social worker!'

I couldn't hold it in any longer. A white-hot rage engulfed me as I continued to scream accusations in her face. But Sister refused to be drawn into an argument.

'Here,' she said, rummaging a hand inside her bag. 'I brought you these.'

She held out her hand and I spotted three packets of Major cigarettes.

'Have you brought me those to keep me quiet?' I sneered, taking them from her. 'Are they supposed to make up for you putting me in here? They treat us like slaves! How could you do that to me, after what happened at Castlepollard? I'm pregnant, for heaven's sake! How could you put me in a place like this?'

Sister clenched both hands together. 'As I said, Mary, I had no choice in the matter. The decision was not mine to make. All I've ever tried to do was help you, child. You know that.'

'Do I? Like the time you hit me in school when I'd damaged my leg so badly that I had to spend months in hospital? Like the time Sister Seraphina "helped" me by throwing me inside Castlepollard? Well, you can take your help and leave. Leave now!' I hollered. 'Leave now, and don't come back because I never want to see you again.'

Sister Celestine sighed heavily as she got to her feet.

'As you wish, child. But I've only ever tried to help you. That's all any of us have tried to do.'

As I watched her go, I knew then that these nuns weren't women. They didn't have the heart of a woman, they had no hearts. They were as cold, cruel, and calculating as the devil himself. They weren't trying to help young mothers like me, they were only interested in one thing, and that was 'selling' our children.

# CHAPTER 18

## Leaving

I'd been 'imprisoned' at High Park for 77 days. I knew this for a fact because I'd chalked each day up inside my head with a feeling of dread it would be followed by another. Soon, 77 days of back-breaking work for no wage or no thanks had felt like 77 years. On the last day, I was called to see Sister just after dinner. I felt nervous walking towards the office because I didn't have a clue what would greet me. By now, I was heavily pregnant at over six months, and the work was proving almost impossible because laundering clothes meant standing on my feet all day.

'Come in,' Sister called, her cold voice giving away nothing of the bombshell she was about to drop.

I walked into the room and closed the door behind me. As I stood there in front of her I searched her face for a clue of what she might be about to say. As usual, she was sat behind her desk poker-faced and impossible to read.

'Now then, Catherine,' she began, shuffling a pile of papers on top of her desk, 'you need to go and pack up your things, because you leave today.'

'Today?' I repeated, as though I didn't quite believe it.

Sister finally raised her head and looked at me sternly. 'Yes, today. Now, you only have ten minutes or so, so you need to move along.'

She gave a wave of her hand as though I was dismissed. But I refused to move because I wanted an explanation. Besides, I'd already been tricked twice, so I had no intention of being tricked again.

'Why am I leaving? I mean, where am I going to?'

Sister kept her eyes on me the whole time as though she was trying to make me feel uncomfortable, but I refused to be intimidated. I demanded an answer because it was the very least I deserved.

'Dunboyne. You're leaving to go to Dunboyne to have your baby.'

I nodded. Dunboyne Castle was where I was supposed to go in the first place.

'That will be all,' Sister added with an impatience that signalled she wanted me to leave.

My heart thudded inside my chest with excitement. I was getting out of this hellhole at last. With very little possessions I'd packed within seconds, throwing my things into a paper bag. I sat on a chair in the hallway by the main entrance and waited. Shortly afterwards, a long black car pulled up outside. There was a small nun sat behind the wheel with another beside her, and there were two more Sisters sat in the back. It was as though they expected trouble and had come mob-handed.

'Catherine,' one of the High Park nuns called, beck-oning me over towards the door.

I looked at her defiantly as she turned the handle and opened the door to the world outside.

'It's Mary. My name is Mary,' I corrected as I walked past her and headed towards the car.

As I approached the two nuns who'd been sitting on the back seat climbed out and left the car door open for me to climb into the middle. I still had my hand on the edge of the door when I heard one of them speak to the nun from High Park.

'Do we give her any money?' she asked as her eyes flitted over towards me.

'No, shush!' Sister hissed.

It was quite clear that they'd been given money for me but intended to keep every penny to themselves. I knew in that moment I was doomed. I guessed Dunboyne Castle would just be a swap – a change of scenery – from High Park. It would still be an institution, just one with a different backdrop. The journey there was just over ten miles. This confirmed something – the driver hadn't needed to stop overnight and rest on my initial journey from Ballina. We'd only been ten miles short of our destination. I'd been lied to, again. I'd been abandoned at High Park and left to my own fate. Sister Celestine and Mrs Elroy had both known what they were doing that night. I'd been left at the Magdalene Laundry, even though I was pregnant, to work and be punished for my 'sins'. In total, the journey took around 40 minutes and that was only because of traffic delays in Dublin city centre. No one said a word to me as I clutched my bag of baby clothes that I'd bought on my hospital appointment 'visits'. Instead of talking, the nuns prayed – no doubt for me and my wretched soul.

It was a relief when we pulled up outside Dunboyne Castle in County Meath, and I was finally able to climb out of the car and escape the oppressive atmosphere within. I looked up and noticed an old-fashioned building that had seen better days. It wasn't how I'd imagined a castle to look because this building looked more like a ramshackle house. As I stretched out my spine, one of the nuns appeared beside me and urged me to follow her to the entrance of a modern two-storey block that was attached to the main building. Although it was called Dunboyne Castle, I later discovered it was more commonly known as Dunboyne Mother-and-Baby Home for Unmarried Mothers. The door opened and we were greeted by another nun, who ushered me to a chair inside the hallway, where I was told to wait.

'Someone will be with you in a moment.'

Moments later, a girl appeared and led me along the corridor towards a small kitchenette on the left, where she made me a cup of tea. The room was full of pregnant girls, all chatting and making hot drinks.

'Where have you come from?' the girl whispered, as she spooned sugar into my tea.

'Ballina, but they've just brought me from High Park in Dublin.'

Her eyes widened as she looked at me in horror. She was just about to say something when the first nun reappeared in front of us.

'Do you have a name?' she asked, without a hint of warmth.

'Yes, it's Mary.'

She shook her head dismissively. 'No, do you have a middle name?'

'Yes, it's Catherine.'

'Well, from now on you are Catherine. Have you got that?'

I felt my heart sink into the pit of my stomach. *Here we go again*, I thought.

'Now, girls,' she said, clapping her hands together to get their attention, 'this is Catherine.'

I blushed as I felt a dozen pairs of eyes look at me and then down at my swollen stomach as though they were trying to guess when I was due. A short while later I was taken to a dormitory containing six or eight beds.

'This will be your bedroom until your baby is born,' I was informed.

Most other girls would have begun to cry at this point, but I felt numb. These surroundings seemed all too familiar because this was how my life had been – a conveyor belt of hospitals and institutions. I'd spent most of my childhood inside hospital before being 'imprisoned' at Castlepollard and High Park. I'd been treated like a slave at the Magdalene Laundry, so, by comparison, Dunboyne seemed like the Hilton because we didn't have to work outside of our usual chores. These included scrubbing, waxing, and buffing the floor, and working in the kitchen. One of my initial 'chores' had been to cook for the girls of Dunboyne, but as soon as I started, I realised it was the worst job in there because your 'working day' didn't finish until well after 3pm. If nothing else, by now I'd learned how to survive, so when asked to cook, I purposefully burned the food and added too much salt and pepper.

'Urrghh!' one of the nuns shrieked, pulling a disgruntled face as she tasted some soup I'd made. 'Can you not cook, girl?'

I shook my head. Of course, I could cook perfectly well, but I didn't want her or anyone else to know that. Afterwards, I was demoted from cook to tea-maker, which didn't bother me in the slightest because it was much quicker to make tea than dinner for 40.

Bizarrely, I also felt a little grateful because I realised that I was more fortunate than most. Unlike the other places, Dunboyne afforded a certain kind of freedom. Girls were allowed to leave and go shopping in the village or even venture out to Dublin, which was only a bus ride away. At that time there was a popular television show called *The Riordans*, and the village of Dunboyne and its surrounding areas were used as the backdrop for a fictional one called Leestown. Although we were allowed to venture out, many girls wouldn't for fear of being captured in the background, pregnant and unmarried. In short, they were in hiding and some had paid to go to Dunboyne to have their babies in secret. I didn't care, because everyone knew I was pregnant, so I felt I had nothing to lose. If you were lucky enough to have money coming in, be it from family or friends, then Dunboyne was a pleasant place to be. Fortunately for me, I still had money in my bank account. Not that I shared this with the nuns. I'd realised how money-obsessed they were and I had no intention of handing over my only lifeline.

There was one teenage girl at Dunboyne who had nothing, only the clothes she stood up in. I don't know what her real name was, but her 'house name' was Oonagh.

'Do you want to come to Dublin with me?' I asked one day.

Oonagh shook her head. 'I haven't any money.'

'What? Not even the bus fare?'

'No, nothing. Not a penny,' she said, casting her eyes downwards.

Oonagh explained that she was from Cork, and had been put in Dunboyne by her family to have her baby.

'But they won't let me keep it. I've to give it up for adoption.'

My heart melted, because in that poor wretch of a girl I recognised part of myself.

'Come on,' I said, grabbing her coat and passing it to her.

'Where are we going?' she asked, pulling it on as I marched off down the corridor.

'I'm taking you to Dublin. I'm going to buy you some clothes for your baby.'

Oonagh stopped in her tracks. 'But I have no money. I can't afford to pay you back…'

I stopped and turned to face her. 'I don't care. I don't want your money, I just want you to have some clothes for your baby.'

A smile broke across her face as she beamed up at me. 'What? And you'd do that for me?'

'Absolutely!' I insisted.

That afternoon, we stepped off the bus in Dublin and walked from one shop to another, searching for the finest baby clothes money could buy. Oonagh's face lit up as she cooed at all the lovely things.

'But I don't know if I'm having a boy or a girl,' she said, unable to choose.

'Just pick out something in a colour that they both can wear. Choose whatever you want.'

With full bags and a successful shopping trip behind us, we stepped on to the bus and headed back towards Dunboyne.

'Thanks, Catherine,' she beamed as the bus made its way along the road.

I leaned in close towards her. 'My name is Mary, but shush!' I whispered, putting a finger against my mouth. 'Don't tell anyone.'

I knew that Oonagh's baby would be adopted, and later, when she gave birth to a little girl, sure enough she was. The nuns had already stripped us of both our names and identities, and I wanted Oonagh to be able to say goodbye to her baby in adoption clothes that she had chosen. Shortly afterwards, Oonagh left Dunboyne. With her baby gone there was little point in her being there any more, but I have never forgotten her or the child she was forced to give away.

There was another girl at Dunboyne, called Helen. She was only 13 years old, but like the rest of us, Helen was heavily pregnant. Sadly, she also had learning difficulties.

'I'm having my baby doll soon,' she told me, cradling her hands around her stomach as a child would do.

Helen was unable to comprehend she was having a real-life baby, never mind becoming a mother.

'I think Helen must have been raped,' one of the girls whispered. 'I mean, look at her, she's still a child. She wouldn't understand what sex with a man was.'

It struck me that she was probably right because Helen also struggled to understand the concept of work. In the end, the nuns moved her somewhere else to give birth to her baby. I still wonder to this day whatever became of her.

There was a minibus at Dunboyne that would come and take girls to and from the maternity hospital in Dublin for check-ups. Sister Anne would drive the bus and order the other girls to wash it so that it gleamed. One day, Sister came to collect a dozen girls, leaving 15 of us behind, including me. With the place virtually empty, I went for a wander along the corridor. I stumbled upon a wooden door that led to a tunnel underneath the convent and the main front door. Normally, this area was out of bounds, but with no one around I decided to take a further look. The tunnel was long, with lots of different doors leading off it. I tried a door to my right, but it was locked. Checking over my shoulder, I walked on a little further. I'd only taken a few more steps when I spotted something hanging from a nail outside one of the doors – it was a bunch of keys. Taking one, I tried it in various locks until I found one that fitted. I turned the large metal key until the lock clicked open. The room inside was dark so I patted a hand along the wall, trying to locate a light switch.

'Got you!' I said, jubilantly flicking it on.

As light flooded the room, my eyes scoured it, taking in all the contents. There were suitcases – dozens of them – stuffed full of women's and girls' clothes. I opened one case after another, but all I discovered were discarded clothes. I found a beautiful blue cotton top and held it up against myself. It'd been so long since I'd worn nice clothes, and standing there in my maternity rags I realised that I wanted the pretty blue top badly. I left it draped on the side as I searched through another dozen or so cases in front of me. It was as though their owners had left in a rush, abandoning their belongings. I felt uneasy and slammed the last case shut, clicking the lock across it.

*Who did all these clothes belong to? Were they the clothes of other expectant mums, like me, who had given birth and then left? If so, why had they left their things behind? Maybe they'd once belonged to the nuns?*

A cold shudder ran down my spine.

*Maybe they belonged to women who'd died during childbirth?*

*No,* I thought, dismissing the notion as soon as I'd considered it. *There are far too many cases for that.*

But the clothes and suitcases dumbfounded me. I continued into the room, where I found some cardboard boxes full of cottons and threads, all unused. I ran my hand through the different colours and wondered why they'd never been given to us, especially when there were girls like Oonagh, who had nothing. I glanced back and spotted the blue top I'd left on the side.

*Surely they wouldn't notice or miss one item of clothing? No,* I reasoned. *Of course they wouldn't.*

Grabbing the top, I clicked off the light and locked the door behind me. Once I was back in the dorm, I swapped my old grey top for the beautiful blue one. By wear alone I'd made it mine, and now I intended to keep it.

Later that day, Sister Anne returned in the minibus.

'You girls can go and clean it, and make sure it's gleaming!' she said with a wagging finger.

As we filed past her, I felt a hand rest against my shoulder.

'Where did you get that top?' Sister asked, eyeing me suspiciously.

'Erm, I found it.'

But I knew from the look on her face I'd been rumbled.

*Maybe the top had once belonged to her?*

'Where? Where did you find it?' she demanded to know.

'Downstairs. I found a door underneath the convent. Then I found another that had been left ajar, so I went in, and there it was.'

Sister's face changed as though a thundercloud had passed overhead.

'Take it off! Take it off right now!' she snapped, pulling at it.

I shook my head defiantly – I was sick of being told what to do.

'No. No, I won't! I found it, and it doesn't belong to anybody here, so I'm going to keep it.'

My voice was loud and raised, and I could tell I was making her feel uncomfortable.

*Maybe there was something behind all the clothes and suitcases that the nuns didn't want anyone to know about?*

I could certainly tell from her startled reaction that I had the upper hand, even if I didn't know or understand why.

'It doesn't belong to anyone here, so why shouldn't I keep it? If I knew who it belonged to then I'd give it back.'

Sister Anne thought for a moment and weighed up the situation. 'All right then, keep it. But not another word, understand?'

I smiled and agreed. It had only been a small victory, but I'd just fought an impossible war, and for once I'd won.

# CHAPTER 19

## The Baby Snatchers

During the final couple of weeks of my pregnancy and time at Dunboyne, there were no other births. We'd have a spate of girls having babies with only a few short gaps in between, but now we'd suddenly hit a lull. There weren't any babies kept at Dunboyne, although that had started to change by the time I came to leave. For the first time since the nuns had turned it into a mother-and-baby home in 1955, alteration work began in autumn 1974, to build small cubicles within the dormitories. They allowed a small bed, a shelf, and space for a cot for those girls who were allowed to keep their children. The arrival of cots filled me with hope.

*Maybe I'd be able to keep my baby, after all?*

My dreams were dashed by a nun after she'd over-heard me asking about the mother-and-baby cubicles.

'It is not an option for you, Catherine. Your baby is going for adoption. Once it is born you should refuse to handle it, boy or girl. Do not feed it, otherwise you might get attached to it. As you know, no one will want you if you have a child. This is your third, so no man will want you, no one.'

I knew she was wrong, but I didn't argue. I also knew this place was nothing like Castlepollard, because at Dunboyne you were sent to hospital to give birth, so there was no way of buying yourself or your child out of the situation. It was the beginning of October 1974, and I was due to give birth any day, so I didn't want to jeopardise anything at this late stage. I was sent to Holles Street Hospital in Dublin for an examination, and the following day, I was given an enema and something to induce labour. By midnight, searing contractions ripped through my body. I knew now it'd only be a matter of time before I held my child in my arms. I could barely wait. But the midwife who'd been assigned to me was dismissive to the point of being rude. She'd refused to give me painkillers, but wouldn't offer an explanation why.

'But I'm in agony. Surely there must be something you can give me to help with the pain?' I begged.

'Just push,' she barked without a hint of compassion in her voice.

But I'd been pushing for hours and I was totally exhausted.

'I'm trying, but I'm worn out,' I sobbed.

'Push!'

'I told you, I'm trying!'

'You're not trying hard enough. Try again!'

I tried to push, but the midwife told me I was pushing the baby out 'wrong'.

'I'm trying my best, but I'm just so tired...' I wept as tears streamed down my face. However, instead of sympathy I felt a short, sharp slap against my face.

'Shut up! Do you hear me? Just shut up!'

For a moment I was stunned into silence. The midwife had just hit me, she'd slapped me across the face.

'That was for your own good,' she insisted as she realised what she'd done. 'Now stay there while I go and fetch you a trolley.'

I lay on the bed dumbfounded and placed a hand against my reddened cheek.

*She's just hit me. The midwife has just hit me for no reason at all.*

And that's when everything came into sharp focus – she was just as bad as the nuns. To her I was an unmarried mother, and therefore a piece of trash that didn't deserve an ounce of her respect. It was clear she thought I wasn't worthy of her time, never mind worthy of being a mother. I'd never felt so alone. There was no Mr or Mrs Campbell, no one to fight my corner, I was alone and in no position to fight back.

At 7am, following a full night of labour, my gorgeous baby girl was born. Weighing in at 9lb 1oz, I'd given birth naturally with no painkillers or stitches for my wounds. But my daughter was absolutely beautiful, with strawberry blonde curls. She was so big at birth that she looked as though she was already three months old. I felt a sense of pride at having brought such a beautiful and strong baby into the world. With her in my arms I felt infallible.

'You treated me like dirt,' I said, looking over towards the midwife as she cleaned up after the birth. 'You hit me, and then you refused me painkillers when I needed them. I'm going to make a formal complaint against you, I'm going to call Matron over this.'

The nurse picked up a bloodied sheet and folded it in her hands. 'You do that. But I'll tell her what I told you, it was for your own good. Someone had to bring you back round.'

Although her face was poker-straight, I noticed that her hands were trembling and I knew then I had her rattled. It was enough for me – the threat that I'd report her – and I would, as soon as I was back on my feet. However, my plan was forgotten later the same morning when three people came into my room to speak with me. There were two men in suits and a woman, who was clutching an official-looking piece of paper in her hand.

'This is a form for your baby that you'll need to pay for. We need money. It'll be six shillings and seven,' she announced, holding out her hand.

I was taken aback by their sudden arrival – my baby was only a few hours old – and I was tired and groggy through lack of sleep. I was so exhausted that I didn't think to ask what the form was for.

'I just need to find my purse,' I agreed, reaching over towards the side table to look for my bag.

'Good,' the woman replied, as she picked up a fountain pen and settled down on a chair next to my bed. 'Now, what's the baby's name to be?'

'Zada,' I told her.

The lady peered over, her face a little flummoxed.

'And how do you spell that?'

'Z... A... D... A,' I said, spelling each letter out slowly.

She glanced up again.

'What a lovely and unusual name. But sorry, could you spell it for me again?'

I did. But it didn't matter because she asked me to spell it out another four or five times.

'All right, I think I've got it now,' she said finally.

I breathed a sigh of relief.

'Now, could you just sign it down here?'

'Could I just have a read?' I asked, fearing this silly woman had spelt my daughter's name wrong.

'No, no, it doesn't matter! Just sign here,' she said, hurrying me along.

'But I haven't looked at it properly...'

'Just sign here,' she repeated, tapping a finger on the bottom part. 'Just put your name here.'

So I did as I was told. I just wanted them out of my room so that I could spend some quality time with my baby daughter.

'Good,' she said, rising to her feet.

I hadn't realised then, but I'd just signed my daughter's birth certificate. It wasn't until over 42 years later that I discovered not only had it been her birth certificate, but the lady, whoever she was, had changed my daughter's name from Zada to Rochelle Creighton. I'd been 'tricked' again. Once she had my signature on the bottom, she could make up whatever name she chose. I'd effectively already started the process of signing away my third child.

I recalled how Sister Celestine had warned me not to become too attached to my baby, but it was too late now because I already was.

*'It'll do you no good in the long run, child. Don't you go getting yourself too emotionally attached to it.'*

Now her words haunted me as I cradled my baby girl in my arms. I'd been warned that if I tried to fight for custody, social services would take her from me as they'd done my other two girls. It seemed as though I would be fighting a losing battle. Keep the child and have it taken anyway, or hand her over and lose her anyway. I was caught in a no-win situation. By the fifth day I decided it was too emotionally painful for me to nurse her any longer. The thought of handing her over was almost too much to bear. So, when the nurse brought her to me, I took a heartbreaking decision.

'Please don't bring her to me any more. I can't nurse her and then give her away.'

Although it had almost broken me in two, I tried to convince myself it was for the best because I had no other option. Neither I nor the Campbells could buy me out of this situation. It was 1974, and there was no such thing as counselling. Once I'd given birth, the hospital was keen to get rid of me and free up another bed on the maternity wing. There wasn't even a follow-up post-natal examination; instead, I was let back out on to the street like vermin. I left my little girl with the clothes I'd bought for her the day I'd escaped the bomb attack in Dublin. I'd hoped they'd somehow bring her luck in her life. With nowhere else left to go, I went back to the place I called home – Ballina. As soon as I arrived, word travelled fast and within hours, Sister Celestine came to visit me at my friend Brenda's house.

'You need to sign the baby over for adoption, Mary. It'll not work out otherwise. Things won't work out for you because no man will want you,' Sister insisted.

Even though my child was currently in foster care, I didn't want to sign her over for adoption, especially not to the two-faced bitches that had controlled me and made my life a misery since I'd been a small child. After the Dublin bombing, I suffered from panic attacks, so her constant harassment of me made me more anxious. Then I received a letter. It was from High Park, asking me to return to the Magdalene Laundry, because I was 'a good worker'.

'What is it, Mary?' Mrs Campbell asked, coming over to me.

I screwed up the letter in my hands, opened up the Aga door, and threw it in the fire. I had no intention of ever returning to that hellhole and I was certain that no one would make me. Instead I only stayed a couple more weeks before leaving again. I headed to the only place I'd ever felt safe and sailed out to sea with some sailors. I'd met a Dutch sailor, who told me his ship was about to sail through Irish waters, just off Galway. He asked the captain if I could board and he'd agreed, so I leapt at the chance to escape. I knew the nuns couldn't find or follow me out to sea, but as the weeks turned into months, I realised I'd eventually have to travel home and face the music. With Christmas fast approaching, I disembarked the ship at Dublin and hitched a lift to Galway, on the west coast of Ireland. That evening, I booked myself into a hotel and caught a train back to Ballina the following day. I'd felt so anxious about going home that I suffered a massive panic attack on the train. It was so frightening that I convinced myself I was having a heart attack.

'Are you all right, Miss?' a gentleman asked as I clutched a hand against my chest and tried to focus on my breathing.

'Yes,' I lied. 'I'm grand, thank you.'

But I wasn't. I was beginning to panic because I knew what awaited me. On 26 December, I walked back into my hometown, and although I was a bag of nerves, I held my head up high. It was quarter past five in the afternoon when I knocked on the door of the Campbells' house.

'Mary,' Mrs Campbell said, her eyes lighting up with joy as soon as she saw me.

Pulling me to her, she hugged me for all I was worth, before holding me at arm's length so that she could take me all in.

'Where on earth have you been, child? I've been so worried. We all have.'

'It's a long story,' I mumbled, exhausted from my journey.

'Well, come in, come in,' she said, taking the bag from my hands. 'Sit down and warm yourself by the fire, while I make us a nice pot of tea. Then you can tell me all about it.'

The kettle hadn't even boiled when there was another knock at the door. Mrs Campbell seemed puzzled as though she wasn't expecting anyone, but went to answer it all the same. Her face fell when she found Sister Celestine standing on her doorstep.

'Sister,' she said curtly, 'and what can I do for you?'

'I'm here to see Mary,' she said, pushing past her and into the room.

Moments later, Sister was standing in front of me. I'd expected her to ask me where I'd been, but she didn't care because she only had one thing in mind.

'Mary, you need to come with me. You need to come over to the convent,' she said, passing me my coat.

'Why? What for?'

'I'll explain more when we get there. Now, come on, and not another moment to waste.'

To this day, I still don't know why I went along with her. Maybe it was down to all those years of being institutionalised – all those years of nuns telling me what to do? Maybe they'd brainwashed me?

In spite of myself, I took my coat, pushed past Mrs Campbell, and followed Sister along the road and down to the convent.

'Follow me into the chapel, child.'

'Are you going to tell me what this is all about?' I asked, stopping in my tracks.

'I've got an appointment. I made it for you. It's about the baby.'

The word 'baby' felt like a stab wound to my heart.

*They'd already taken my daughter, what else did they want from me?*

'What about her? What about Zada?'

Sister looked confused for a moment as I mentioned the name, but shook her head as though it didn't matter.

'It's about the baby and the adoption. I've made an appointment, but we don't have long, so we've got to hurry.'

'Why? What time is the appointment?' I asked.

'Six thirty.'

I glanced at my watch.

'But it's ten past six now.'

Sister Celestine looked over with a determined look on her face.

'I know, that's why we need to make a move.'

All sorts of thoughts and concerns swirled inside my head as we walked towards the solicitor's private residence. I wondered what would happen if I refused to sign? Probably nothing. The nuns had this whole adoption racket sewn up. Any unwillingness to sign on my part would probably count for nothing.

'You've really got no option, Mary,' Sister said, breaking my thoughts.

She could tell from my face that I was having doubts.

Moments later, I robotically scrawled my name at the bottom of some official papers: I'd just lost a third baby. Suddenly, the reality of what I'd done hit me like a ton of bricks as emotion overwhelmed me and I broke down.

'What have I done? What have I done?' I gasped.

'For heaven's sake, pull yourself together, child,' Sister snapped.

The solicitor looked up at her a little shocked, so she tried again, this time in a much softer voice.

'You've done the right thing, Mary,' she cooed, patting my back gently.

But it didn't feel right. Nothing felt right, or even real any more. I was caught up in the middle of a nightmare. I also knew that I couldn't win. If I hadn't signed then my daughter would have been fostered until I did. I had no other option because they hadn't given me one.

'I think I want her back,' I said, changing my mind. 'I want my baby back!'

But Sister refused to listen to another word. Instead, she asked the solicitor if she could use his phone.

'May I?' she asked, picking up the receiver.

'Be my guest, Sister,' he said, resting back in his chair.

Through my tears, I watched as she dialled a number and waited for someone to answer the other end.

'I've got Mary Creighton here, and she's in a terrible state. Please may I bring her to see you?'

She nodded as the voice spoke, replying to her question.

'Very well. Thank you, Doctor.'

Once we were outside in the cold street, the enormity of my situation hit me hard.

'I want her back. I can't lose another baby,' I wept, as I walked numbly up the street towards the doctor's house.

The doctor examined me and asked what was wrong, but I couldn't even begin to articulate my feelings of loss. Instead, he and Sister Celestine chatted quietly as I sat and sobbed. Before too long, a decision had been made.

'Mary, I'm waiting for a private hospital taxi to take you to hospital for a couple of days. Do you understand?' the doctor told me.

I did, but I was still so distraught that I couldn't absorb what he was telling me.

Shortly afterwards, I pulled up at a building where I was injected with something that was meant to calm me down. Then I was given some small white pills. The following morning, I was awoken by the swish of the hospital curtains as someone pulled them open around my bed. A man in a tweed jacket stood in front of me. I shifted uneasily, because he was a dead ringer for Dr Crippen from the horror movies.

He glanced down at a sheet of paper in his hand, checking my name as he read it aloud. 'Miss Creighton, I'm going to give you an internal examination.'

I was stunned because it'd been almost three months since I'd given birth.

'Excuse me, but are you a gynaecologist?' I asked, expecting him to say yes.

'No, I'm a psychiatrist.'

I pushed my hands flat against the mattress and dragged myself into a sitting position.

'Well, you're not going to give me an internal. You're not a gynaecologist, so why would I let you?'

Nothing made sense any more, but I was certain of one thing: I'd had enough of people telling me what to do. I'd been too trusting all my life, but not any more.

'What's wrong?' I asked, climbing out of bed and pulling my clothes on. 'Didn't you maul your wife last night? Because I'll tell you this, you're not going to maul me!'

The doctor didn't say a word as I ran out of the ward and through several doors. Eventually, I reached a sitting room, and, with trembling hands, I flopped down into one of the chairs and lit up a cigarette. I inhaled the smoke deeply to try and calm my nerves.

*What has my life become?* I wondered as I blew a cloud of blue-grey smoke up into the air.

I glanced down at my watch; it was only 10.30 in the morning, yet my nerves were already in tatters. I'd just lit up my second cigarette when two nurses appeared.

'Mary?' one asked gently.

I nodded.

'You need to come with us.'

I wasn't sure where they would take me, but I figured I'd rather go with them than back up to the ward with the creepy-looking doctor.

'Where are we going?'

'You'll see when we get there,' the nurse said, linking her arm through mine.

Dazed and confused, I allowed myself to be led back into the hospital and along a corridor. We passed through several sets of doors, but as we reached the last set, she pulled out a set of keys and unlocked it.

'Wait here,' one of the nurses said.

I glanced around the room, which had four tables inside it. Around 15 or 20 women were seated at the tables, staring out into space as though they'd been drugged. It was obvious they were patients of some kind. There were plant pots that had been placed on each table in a bid to make the room look cheery, but instead, they made it look grim. The windows were situated high up on the walls – too high up to peer out. I shuddered because they reminded me of the high windows in the dorm at High Park. I waited for ten minutes while the nurse handed out cigarettes to the patients from the drawer of a cheap white desk. Without warning, a door on my left creaked opened and the doctor from the last ward popped his head around the corner of it.

'Miss Creighton, come with me.'

My heart was thudding violently as I followed him. I walked into a room that contained eight beds, and noticed a girl lying on one of them. She was almost naked and sprawled out at an awkward angle across it. In fact, she was so still that for a moment I wondered if she was dead. My heart was pumping furiously, setting my senses on high alert. There was no nurse, only me, the doctor, and the unconscious girl. I watched as he proceeded to open his doctor's bag. He pulled out a long glass syringe, which looked strangely old-fashioned, and drew some amber liquid up into it.

'What's the name of that medicine?' I demanded to know.

I suddenly felt hot and claustrophobic in that little room with the doctor and the unconscious girl. He looked over at me fleetingly as he continued to draw the liquid slowly into the needle.

'You don't need to know.'

But I was determined I wouldn't be tricked or silenced again: 'If you're going to inject me with it I need to know what it's called in case I'm allergic to it.'

'Paraldehyde,' he said, stepping forward. He lifted the needle and pierced my skin, as he plunged the liquid into my bloodstream.

'I will fix you,' he whispered, as the room turned black and my mind faded to nothing.

# CHAPTER 20

# The Mental Hospital

I was admitted to a mental hospital on 27th December 1974, but I don't remember it or anything that followed for a couple of days after the doctor had injected me. The medicine he'd administered had been strong and hallucinogenic, similar to how I'd imagined LSD to be, and it had worked with immediate effect. By the time I eventually came round, a nurse was standing by my bed.

'Hello, how are you feeling?' she asked.

Her face zoomed in and out of focus, making me feel dizzy.

'Where am I?'

'Don't you remember?'

I shook my head and tried to perch myself up on my elbows, but my body felt like a lead slab.

'I don't remember much. That doctor injected me with something... something strong.'

The nurse sighed. I noticed her check over her shoulder before she replied: 'Yes, we were a little shocked at how you were treated, I mean. There was no need because you came into Room 113, and you just stood there, not moving.'

It was all coming back to me. 'That's right,' I said, lifting myself up.

The fair-haired nurse reached behind me and plumped up my pillow to make me more comfortable.

'Normally, the patients that are mentally disturbed go for the plant pots first. That's why they're there, on the tables,' she explained. 'They pick them up and, whoosh! They smash them against the walls or the floor. They even throw them at the high windows, but not you. To be honest, I don't even know why you're here.'

The nurse had seemed friendly so I confided that the same doctor had asked to give me an internal examination. Her face changed and she stopped plumping my pillows and straightened up. It was clear she was visibly shocked, but she didn't answer. But her reaction had given her away. I was clear the internal hadn't been a normal request. However, she refused to be drawn into further conversation and urged me to get up, washed, and dressed. I still felt a little shaky on my feet as she led me along the corridor and down towards the dining hall. The hall was massive and full of female patients of differing ages. The deafening noise of cutlery scraping against plates filled the room as the women ate their dinner robotically. There was no chatter or friendly banter, just the noise of metal against pottery. I didn't mind because I was used to the silence. The thought of being locked up didn't faze me, either. But the fact I'd been placed in a mental institution against my will had disturbed me. I was terrified I'd never see daylight again and I'd be locked inside forever, like one of the old women at the Magdalene Laundry.

'Sit here,' the nurse said, pointing down at a hard plastic chair.

I was handed a plateful of food, but the drugs were still in my system so the plate began to zoom in and out of focus just as the nurse had done. I shook my head to try and clear my vision and then tried to pick up my knife and fork. But as I did so, the cutlery moved. It shot across the table as though it'd been attached to an invisible piece of string that someone had pulled for a joke. I stopped, focused, and reached out again, but my knife and fork moved again, spreading away from my plate. I paused, took a deep breath, and slammed a hand hard against the table to try and 'trap' my cutlery so it couldn't scurry away. A dozen pairs of eyes turned to me as I mumbled incoherently and picked them up. But the faces and shapes of people turned from eyes into heads. Then the heads changed into bodies and then black blobs that zoomed in and out of focus.

Women sat at my table grazed at their plates as though they were a herd of farm animals. Gripping my fork, I tried to put the food inside my mouth, but I missed and stabbed the side of my cheek in the process. In the end, I became so frustrated that I ate my dinner straight off the plate with my mouth, like a dog. Afterwards, and with my face smeared with food, I was led back to my ward. I sat on my bed and stared blankly at the wall, wondering where on earth my life would go from here. It wasn't until a few days later I realised the cutlery hadn't moved at all. It was all in my mind – a mind bent out of shape and out of time by hallucinogenic drugs. But the strange sensation – of floating above my own body – lasted for days until it eventually wore off.

One morning, the same doctor reappeared in Room 113. He had another injection for me; the contents were already inside the glass syringe that he'd pulled from his doctor's bag.

'What's that?' I asked, eyeing both it and him suspiciously.

He explained it was a drug I'd have to have injected into my thigh for five days.

'And what happens after five days?'

'Then it will be given orally, along with another tablet.'

Years later, I did an Internet search on the medicine he'd given me. I discovered that both pills were used to treat epileptic fits, something I'd never suffered from. As the needle pierced my skin I wanted to push him away and run. I wanted to escape my new prison. I wanted to do all those things, but I knew it was pointless because the doors were kept locked at all times. Instead, I remained there compliant, like a lamb to the slaughter. After the injection, I was moved to a large open ward. Unlike my other room, this one was unlocked, but it didn't matter because I knew all the outside doors were.

As I was shown my new bed, a nurse explained the rules. 'You mustn't leave this room. You mustn't go over that threshold without permission, do you understand?'

I nodded numbly, my emotions blunted by the medical cosh I'd just received. I was treated like a caged animal by the nurses, nothing more, and nothing less. Deep down, I knew my mind was sound. I realised I was being kept there to 'forget about my child'. The fact I'd been admitted to a mental hospital would probably mean I'd never see her again because I'd now been labelled 'mentally unstable'.

*They've done this to shut me up,* I thought bitterly, as I sat facing the wall.

*The longer I'm in here, the less chance I'll have of ever seeing her again.*

My heart hammered inside my ribcage like a desperate fist knocking against the door of a desolate house. I felt dead – hollowed by the loss of my babies. I'd had three children taken; I had nothing else to lose.

The longer I remained there, the more I realised I wasn't alone. One day, I got talking to an elderly lady called May, who had been a skilled dressmaker in her younger days.

'Why are you in here, May? What happened to you?' I asked as the afternoon stretched out in front of us.

May's eyes misted over and she stared off into the middle distance, lost in thought. She smiled wistfully as though she'd just been reminded of a happy time, then her face clouded over and her eyes dropped down to her lap. Her hands knotted anxiously together.

'I had a baby,' she whispered.

I was flabbergasted. I'd always presumed she was an old spinster.

'I didn't realise you'd been married.'

'I wasn't, that was the problem. I was an unmarried mother, but it was the 1920s, and they didn't know what to do with a girl like me. I was barely a child myself, only 17 years old.' She wrung her hands together.

I gasped. May's story mirrored my own.

'But what about the baby? What happened to your child?'

May lifted her head as the tears flowed freely down her troubled face. 'They took him, Mary. They took him and they put me in here.'

I fell back in my chair as though she'd just slapped me.

'What? And you've been here ever since?'

She nodded.

'But how can they do that? How can they put you in a mental hospital for having a baby?' My voice was incredulous.

The old lady shrugged and looked down at her hands as though she was ashamed.

'It's what they did back then. Out of sight, and out of mind, I suppose.'

'And you've never been outside? I mean, they've never let you out of here?'

'No.'

'But they can't do that. I mean, why don't you ask them to let you go?' I gestured over to the whitewashed plaster walls. 'This isn't a prison. They can't do that to you.'

May glanced up. 'But where would I go, child? I'm an old woman, this is all I know.'

She had been locked up for almost 50 years, just for having a child.

*I thought my life was bad*, I said to myself as I considered the frail old lady before me.

Although her story had been shocking, it turned out that it wasn't unique. As with the Magdalene Laundry, I met other women who'd been put in there by their husbands, who'd said they were crazy, when what they actually had was post-natal depression. The fathers had either kept their child or given it away for adoption. Now, with his 'old wife' locked up in a mental institution, the man was free to marry again. I felt blessed that I'd been born later.

I thought about my own situation and became convinced the doctor had been in cohorts with the nuns. I was certain they'd conspired to have me locked away so I'd never see my baby again. I wondered if I was suffering from paranoia, but when I heard May's story and similar ones, I realised I probably wasn't. I wasn't the first victim of the 'system', and, sadly, I wouldn't be the last.

I was injected in my thigh for five days, and on the sixth, I received the same dose but in tablet form. The drugs had left me in a semi-comatose state until I felt nothing. My body had felt so numb, I was certain you could've stuck pins in me and I wouldn't have felt a thing. Every day I asked the nurses the same question – when would I be allowed out?

'Not today, Mary. Maybe tomorrow, Mary,' they'd repeat like a broken record. 'The doctor says you're not ready to leave just yet.'

This constant daily routine had lasted for almost a month until one day I asked the doctor the same question.

'Now, Miss Creighton, I am allowing you out for the weekend,' he told me unexpectedly.

My mouth hung open with shock. I couldn't even speak, so the doctor filled the silence.

'But first, you must wait for the nurse with your medication. It is Friday, so you can leave today, but you will come back here on Sunday evening before six o'clock, do you understand?'

'Yes,' I said, my voice barely a whisper.

'You will come back now, won't you?' he asked, repeating himself again and again.

I nodded, but I'd stopped listening to him because inside my head I was already plotting my escape.

# CHAPTER 21

## Liverpool

Half an hour later, the nurse came over to see me. In her hand she had two off-white boxes, edged with black. Each box contained 100 tablets, making 200 pills for just two days. I'd just been handed suicide on a plate.

'The doctor says you're to take your tablets regularly,' the nurse said, when I wondered why I'd been given so many pills.

I only took two tablets a day, something didn't add up. I could have left the hospital and, if I'd felt that way inclined, downed the lot of them with a bottle of booze. But I'd done that before, and I had no intention of going down that particular path ever again.

'I'll be sure to take them,' I agreed, slipping both boxes in my bag. I would have said anything to escape that ward, the doctor, and the hospital.

I stood back and watched as the nurse unlocked the door and led me out into the main reception area.

'Look after yourself, Mary. And we'll see you on Sunday night.'

I smiled and nodded, even though I had no intention of ever setting foot inside that hospital again. Once outside, I walked over to the railway station and caught a train back to Ballina. As soon as I'd stepped off the train I headed straight to the bank. I'd need every penny I had if my plan was going to work. With the cash safely tucked inside in my handbag, I went to my friend Brenda's house.

'Mary!' she gasped as soon as she saw me.

'Please don't say a word to anyone, Brenda,' I whispered as I stepped inside. 'I've not been here and you've not seen me, if anyone asks.'

Brenda seemed taken aback.

'Er, all right. But what's happened? Where have you been?'

I sat down and told Brenda everything. I told her how I'd signed my daughter over to the nuns, and when I'd changed my mind, I'd been locked up in a mental hospital. Her eyes widened with horror as she listened to my sorry story.

'It's just... I'm... well, I don't know what to say, Mary. It's wicked what they've done to you.'

I leaned forward and grabbed her hands in mine.

'That's why you can't tell anyone, Brenda. You mustn't tell anyone I've been here. Please promise me you won't.'

'Of course I won't. You're my friend, Mary. We've always been friends and we always will be. I'll keep your secret. The nuns won't get anything out of me,' she said, shaking her head and tapping a hand against her chest.

With tears in my eyes, I stood up and hugged her. It felt good to have a friend, and right now, Brenda felt like my only friend on earth.

'But where will you go? What will you do?' she asked, pulling away from me.

'I don't know, but I need to leave Ireland. And I need to leave in the morning before they come looking for me.'

That evening, to celebrate my new freedom, I decided to nip out to the local pub. I realised the nuns wouldn't be in there, and by the time they'd heard I had been I'd be long gone. I was standing at the bar when I spotted a Portuguese sailor called Adao, who I knew from my days in Liverpool.

'Mary!' he called, waving his hand in the air to beckon me over. 'I didn't know you were back in Ireland. Come here and have a drink with me.'

'I'm not staying. I'm just here for the night, Adao,' I insisted.

'Why? Where you go?' he asked with a quizzical look on his face.

'Ah, that,' I said, tapping my hand against the bar, 'is the secret.'

Adao smiled. I knew he'd always had a soft spot for me – and I had one for him too. He was a lovely man and I was a woman starved of love, so, when he put his arm around me, I didn't remove it. I was searching for love, and that night I didn't care who I sought comfort from. So when one thing led to another, I allowed it to happen. I knew I'd been reckless, but I was sick of doing what everyone told me to do. I'd spent my life doing that, and look where it got me – locked up in shame. But now I refused to feel ashamed or frightened any more. I'd escaped a mother-and-baby unit, and a Magdalene Laundry – both prisons in their own right – only to be locked up inside a mental hospital. I'd three children taken from me, and I felt compelled to abort another. Now I had nothing left to lose.

'We must keep in touch, Mary. Write to me,' Adao insisted as we said goodbye.

I nodded, even though I had no intention of doing so. I'd had enough. From now on, it would be me against the rest of the world.

The following morning, I was up bright and early to catch the first train to Dublin. Walking along the street, I glanced over my shoulder to check that Sister Celestine or Sister Seraphina weren't following me. My pace quickened every time I saw a shadow or heard a noise. I'd been 'taken' from my hometown before, and the nuns had seemed to know my every move. I was terrified they'd find me and ship me back off to the mental hospital, where I'd end up like May, never to be seen again.

Once on the train I still felt nervous. Every time someone passed by my carriage I'd turn my face away and stare out of the window – I couldn't risk anyone seeing me, not at this late stage. I still felt jumpy even as I boarded a boat at Dublin bound for England.

'I'd like a ticket for Liverpool,' I told the man behind the ticket counter.

'Single or return?' he asked.

'Single,' I said, a little too quickly.

The man looked up a little quizzically. 'You sound certain,' he said, chortling.

'Oh, I am. Believe me.'

Only once the ship had cast out far into the Irish Sea did I finally feel safe. I stood on the deck, took a deep breath, and watched my homeland – my beloved Ireland – become a faint line on the horizon. Breathing in the fresh sea air, I exhaled slowly and tried to clear my mind.

*My baby girl is still there. I'm leaving her behind*, I thought sadly.

My heart ached for the baby snatched from me, taken by those I'd been taught to trust the most – the nuns, and the Catholic Church.

*Well, you can't hurt me any longer*, I thought, as the biting wind sliced against the side of my face. *You've done your worst. I have no children because you've stolen them all. You've taken everything, apart from one thing – my freedom.*

My handbag weighed heavy against my shoulder as the boat continued to make its way out into the open sea. Once Ireland had become a speck, I dipped a hand and felt around inside my bag until I'd located them. Wrapping my fingers around the first box, I pulled the first packet out into the cold, afternoon air, and, one by one, emptied them into the palm of my hand. I lifted my hand and scattered the tablets like confetti into the dark inky blue black sea below. They floated momentarily before sinking downwards, disappearing into the depths of the dark water. I took out the second packet and did the same. The pills slipped through my fingers like the passport photographs of the cornflake babies at Castlepollard. All those lost little souls ripped from the arms of their loving mothers. Stolen children, taken away forever.

# CHAPTER 22

## A New Life

Once I'd docked in Liverpool, I travelled to Birkenhead to see Maria. She'd been like a mum to me when I was at my lowest ebb. Maria had saved my life when I'd swallowed bottles of pills after losing my daughters. Now I'd had three children taken from me and I'd been locked up inside a mental hospital, but instead of destroying me, I had been empowered. I realised then that I was a true survivor. I also knew Maria would welcome me with open arms.

'Mary!' she said, embracing me when she saw me on her doorstep. 'What a lovely surprise. What are you doing back in Liverpool?'

I looked up at her, relieved to see a friendly face.

'It's such a long story, I don't know where to begin,' I replied, trying to blink a stubborn tear that had settled in the corner of my eye.

'Well, I'll put the kettle on and you can tell me all about it.'

We talked long into the afternoon. I told Maria all about the hospital and losing a third child.

'They can't just take your baby!' she gasped.

'Well, that's what they did.'

She shook her head in disgust. 'I can't believe how you've been treated, I really can't.'

I looked down at the floor and thought of my lost babies. Tears filled my eyes.

'The thing is, I know I can be a good mother if they'd only give me a chance. They just won't let me, that's why they locked me up inside a mental hospital, so that I couldn't get Zada back. If I go back to Ireland, they'll lock me up again, and I'll be like May.'

'Who's May?' Maria asked as she cradled a steaming hot mug of tea in her hands.

'She's a woman I met inside the hospital. She was an unmarried mother like me, but she had her baby in the twenties. They locked her up and never let her out.'

Maria looked appalled. She placed her mug down on the coffee table in front of her. 'What? And she's still in there now?'

I nodded.

'Yep.'

'But Mary, that's terrible.'

'I know. But there are others – women who've been locked up by their husbands, who say they're mad. They've only done it so they can go off and get remarried. Honestly, Maria, if I end up back inside that hospital with that doctor I swear I'll kill myself. When they find out I've run away, all hell will break loose. But if they find me, they'll lock me up and throw away the key.'

She leaned forward and patted my hand reassuringly.

'Well, you have nothing to fear, because you can stay here.'

'Really?'

'Absolutely.'

And so the decision was made. I could stay with Maria for as long as it took for me to get back on my feet.

It felt good to finally be able to live my life without constantly looking over one shoulder, checking for Sister Seraphina or Sister Celestine. I still kept in touch with both Mrs Campbell and Brenda, ringing them every so often to let them know I was all right.

A short while after I'd arrived at Maria's house, I started to feel sick. To both my utter shock and delight, I realised that I was pregnant again. There was only one person who could be the father, and that was Adao, the Portuguese sailor.

'Maria,' I said, ashen-faced after a particularly severe bout of morning sickness. 'I think I'm pregnant.'

Maria beamed and ran over to give me a hug. 'Mary, that's fantastic news.'

We began to laugh, and then I remembered with a sudden jolt of fear.

*What if they took this child away from me?* I panicked. *I couldn't stand to lose another baby.*

I had to do something and fast. I remembered an African woman I'd met previously in a laundrette. We'd spoken quite a few times while waiting for our laundry to finish. We chatted about everything from the weather to what it felt like to be a stranger in a foreign country. We seemed to have lots of things in common, and eventually we became quite friendly. She confided in me about her Iraqi boyfriend, who was due to be deported. She couldn't marry him herself because she'd already got married to stay in the country.

'But you could,' she insisted at the time.

I'd immediately dismissed it because I knew it was wrong, but every time I saw her after that she would mention it. I'd always laughed it off and thought no more of it until now. I needed to get married so that I could change my name. At first I'd been horrified by her suggestion, but the more I thought about it, the more it made complete sense. By marrying him, he'd gain a passport and I'd gain a different surname, making me virtually untraceable.

*If they can't find me then they can't take my baby.*

A week or so later, on 17 May 1975, I arranged to meet the woman's boyfriend down the local register office. Within half an hour, we'd become man and wife. I was already five months pregnant and had started to show, so to the outside world we looked just like every other shotgun wedding of the 1970s. But following the ceremony, the man changed and became extremely hostile towards me.

'You're my wife now, you do as I say,' he said, grabbing my wrist.

I flinched and pulled away from his grasp.

'Get your hands off me. I'm nobody's property, and I'm certainly not yours!'

But the man was insistent: 'You come with me.'

'No!' I replied, suddenly feeling scared and completely out of my depth.

I watched as he pulled something out from his pocket. It was a knife.

'You come with me,' he said, holding it up towards me.

'All right,' I said to try and placate him. 'But I just need to nip and buy a packet of cigarettes first. There's a shop just around the corner. I won't be long, I promise.'

I'd already started running along the street before he'd had the chance to answer. Dashing through the terraced-lined streets, I ran as fast as I could to get as far away as possible. Panting and struggling for breath, I ran into a corner shop and was still looking over my shoulder in case my 'husband' was following me.

'Are you all right?'

I turned to see the man behind the counter staring straight at me. I must have looked utterly terrified because as soon as he saw the state of me he came dashing out from behind the till to check I was okay.

I was still trying to catch my breath as I tried to explain to him what and who I was running from.

'I-I-I've just done s-s-s-something very stupid,' I gasped as I told him what had just happened.

The man realised I was pregnant and insisted on making me a cup of tea.

'Please,' he said, showing me to a chair behind the till, 'please sit down.'

Soon we were chatting away like old friends. The shopkeeper was called Mohammed, and he was 30 years older than me. Unlike the brute I'd just married, Mohammed was kind, and my instinct – which I'd now come to rely on – told me he was a good person.

'I'm too scared to go home in case him and his girl-friend come looking for me,' I said, beginning to weep.

Mohammed patiently listened to my tale of woe, paused for a moment, and then came up with a suggestion.

'It's not much, and there's no kitchen, but I have some spare rooms upstairs if you'd like to stay in those for a while, just until you get yourself sorted.'

I looked at him in astonishment. I'd only just met him, but I could tell he was genuine.

'But you hardly know me,' I said, dabbing my eyes with a scrunched-up tissue.

'True, I don't. But I know a damsel in distress when I see one. And I see one sitting right here in front of me.'

I began to laugh. 'Okay, but only if you're sure?'

Mohammed smiled. 'I am. In fact, it'd be nice to have a bit of company.'

Mohammed turned out to be exactly the man I thought he'd be – a truly lovely and kind gentleman who neither wanted nor expected anything in return.

I soon settled into my new place. Afterwards, I strolled down to a nearby phone box to call Mrs Campbell and let her know I'd moved.

'Mary,' she gasped. 'I've had a black fella knocking at my door, looking for you. He's Portuguese or something. He says you're having his baby.'

I blushed, and then I reminded myself that I had absolutely nothing to feel ashamed about: it was my body and my life.

'Yes, that's right, I am. But please don't give him my new address, because I don't want a man in my life. I don't want anyone telling me what to do any more.'

However, my words were to prove short-lived because after spending so much time with Mohammed, I realised not all men were the same. He was so kind and generous towards me that it wasn't long before we became a couple.

My daughter, Charlotte, was born in October 1975, exactly one year and six days to the day I'd given birth to my baby girl in Dublin. The same child that had been taken from me by the nuns. But this time, with my new name and new respectability, there was no religion, nuns, or social worker waiting at my bedside to snatch my child away from me. For the first time in my life I finally felt in control of my own future.

'Don't you mind that Charlotte's not your baby?' I asked Mohammed one night when she was a few weeks old.

He took her in his arms and cradled her gently. As she nuzzled in against him, his face lit up and broke into a huge smile. 'No, because I will love her as though she is.'

And he kept his word. As our relationship developed into something more, I found myself pregnant again, but this time with Mohammed's child.

'I will treat them both the same. They will be equal to me.'

And they were. Charlotte was treated exactly the same as her new baby sister, Elizabeth. Mohammed didn't care that we weren't bonded by blood because, in his eyes, we were bonded by something far stronger: love.

With two girls and a loving partner, I finally felt complete. I had two children, and I wouldn't allow anyone to take them away from me. I still continued to suffer panic attacks because I lived with the constant fear that my past would one day catch up with me. I was always waiting for the knock at the door, and a nun or a social worker to come and take my girls.

One day, there was a knock at the door at the side of the shop. Mohammed answered it and called out to me. My heart was in my mouth as I walked downstairs from the flat above, wondering who on earth it could be. But as I peered around the edge of the door my heart felt fit to burst when I was greeted by the sight of my younger brother, Joseph.

'What are you doing here?' I shrieked. I could hardly believe it. I'd not seen him since he was a small child, but I'd recognise his face anywhere.

'I'm living in Liverpool. I've got a girlfriend and everything,' he said with a daft lopsided grin on his face.

'Come in, come in...'

Mohammed looked up at us both a little baffled.

'It's all right,' I said, wrapping my arms around his neck. 'He's my brother.'

Mohammed grinned, shook Joseph's hand, and disappeared back into the shop.

'But how on earth did you find me?'

If Joseph could find me, then anyone could, I thought, beginning to panic.

'Mrs Campbell. But don't worry, I've been sworn to secrecy.' He gave me a cheeky smile and put a finger against his lips.

Joe explained how my aunties and uncle had told the children not to keep in touch with me.

'But I was determined to come and find you, Mary. I never agreed with any of the things they said about you. Not ever.'

I put a hand against my chest as tears began to tumble down my cheeks.

'It's so good to see you again,' I said, my voice choking with emotion.

'You too, sis,' he said, giving me a nudge.

After that first meeting, Joe and I stayed in regular contact. Sometimes he'd come and stay with us, if he happened to be over my side of the city. It felt great to finally have family back in my life, even if it was only one brother.

'What about Mum and Dad?' I asked one afternoon.

Joe shook his head. 'They're still in America, last I heard.'

I had mixed feelings about my mother, but my heart ached for my lovely father because he'd always fought my corner.

'I miss Dad,' I said, feeling quite teary.

Joe looked down. 'Me too,' he admitted.

Life continued, until one day when I became extremely unwell. Crippled with stomach pains, I was rushed to hospital for an emergency D&C to clean out my womb. Tragically, the doctor accidentally cut my womb, which led to internal bleeding and almost cost me my life. I was in such a critical condition that a priest was called in to give me the last rites. Somehow, I pulled through and underwent several operations. But as I came around after the second, I haemorrhaged. I drifted in and out of consciousness as doctors scurried around my bed like mice. But as I lay there, I felt totally calm.

*Please don't worry because I'm going to be all right.*

It was my mind playing tricks on me. In reality, I was critically ill again and barely clinging on to life. The priest arrived, and I was anointed, but I still wasn't ready to die.

*I need to live. I need to get through this. My girls need their mother,* I told myself as I lay there, my life slowly ebbing away.

It was during those crucial hours that I spotted Joe sitting by the side of my bed. Unbeknownst to me, he'd been there for most of the week, willing me to pull through, and that's when a miracle happened. Instead of dying, I began to recover. I'd willed myself to survive – to live for my children – and I'd brought myself back from the brink of death. I needed to live for my girls, not only for the ones I had, but for those I'd lost.

It was a slow recovery, but eventually, I began to improve. After several weeks, I was finally discharged. But the whole terrifying experience – that I could have died and left my children alone – haunted me. The panic attacks I'd suffered since the day of the Dublin bomb came back with a vengeance.

I realised that I needed to start dealing with the mistakes of my past if I had any hope of living a peaceful future. I started by writing a letter to the Home Office informing them my 'marriage' had been a sham. I was interviewed and, because I'd co-operated and told the police everything, I was never charged. Instead, three years later, my fake marriage was annulled.

Sadly, Mohammed and I split and went our separate ways when Elizabeth was seven months old. There were no arguments, and we remained great friends; I'd just come to the realisation that I couldn't be in a relationship because I couldn't stand feeling 'hemmed in'. Sadly, the horrors of my past had begun to affect my future. I'd spent my entire life being told what to do, and now it was my time to be free. Although I moved into my own council house, Mohammed continued to be a great father to both my children.

I was at home one morning in early May 1978 when there was a knock at the door. Kate, a friend of mine, answered it and came upstairs to find me.

'There's a small red-haired woman and a grey-haired man waiting downstairs to see you,' she told me.

I can't explain why, but I knew exactly who it was – it was my mum and dad.

'Could you make them a cup of tea?' I asked, trying to compose myself. 'I'll be right down.'

I'd dreamt of this moment for so long, from when I'd first been put in Castlepollard to my final days in the Magdalene Laundry. I'd passed all those long and lonely hours wishing my parents would come and rescue me. They never had, but now they were here on my doorstep, and, as I was about to find out, they needed my help.

'Dad!' I cried, running into his arms.

He looked as excited as I felt to see me.

'Mary,' he gasped, holding me so close that I thought he'd squeeze the life out of me.

I sensed my mother standing there and knew she was expecting the same reception. To be honest, I'd often wondered how I'd feel when I finally saw her again, but instead of hatred, I felt nothing. I was just so overwhelmed with love for my father.

'When did you get back from America?' I asked, skirting around the issues of the past.

'We've just got back,' said Dad, holding my hand as we sat down.

'But how did you know where to find me?' I asked.

'Joseph, or rather Joe's girlfriend's mother.'

I nodded. News certainly travelled fast. But I didn't care, I was just so thrilled to see Dad again.

'Well, you can stay here, if you like?'

Mum looked shocked by my kindness. I think she'd expected me to show them none, just as she'd done with me all those years before.

'Only if you're sure that would be all right,' Dad insisted, patting my hand. 'We don't want to put you out, or anything.'

I waved a hand in front of me and picked up my tea off the table. 'Of course you can stay here. I insist. I'll just bunk in with the girls.'

And so it was decided: Mum and Dad would come and live with me. Although they were both thrilled to meet their granddaughters, nothing was ever mentioned about the babies that had been taken from me. Secretly, it broke my heart because they'd all been my children – children I had lost. Instead, in true typical Irish fashion, it was swept under the carpet and never spoken of.

My parents continued to stay with me while they were looking for a house of their own, although things were strained between me and my mother.

'What are you going out for?' she demanded to know one evening as I kissed my girls goodbye and headed towards the door for a night out at the cinema with friends.

'Don't worry,' I told her. 'Kate's going to babysit.'

Mum put her hands on her hips and pulled a face in disapproval. 'But don't you think it's a bit late to be going out?'

I pulled on my coat and fastened the buttons, my eyes not leaving hers for a second.

'I've been on my own for a very long time, and I choose when I do and don't go out. It's nothing to do with you, I'm not a child any more.'

With that I closed the door behind me.

I could imagine her standing there, shaking her head in disgust, but she couldn't tell me what to do. She had lost that right when she sent me away to Castlepollard. I was an adult and a mother. Even though I now had my brother and parents around me, I was used to being self-sufficient and not relying on others. She couldn't control me – not any more. She was living in my house, by my rules. For the first time in my life, the tables had turned.

Sadly, four years after we'd split, Mohammed suffered a heart attack and was admitted to hospital. I hadn't realised it at the time, but it had been a warning. A few months later, he suffered a second massive heart attack that killed him on the spot. He was just 53. I grieved for him. Not only had he been a fantastic partner and father, he was one of the kindest men I'd ever know. In many ways, he reminded me of my own father.

Eventually, my parents found a place of their own and they moved out. Life carried on, although I remained single for the next couple of years, until one day when I got talking to a Cantonese man, walking his dog in the park. Heng was a friendly chap, so when he asked me out, I agreed. He already had a two-year-old daughter from a previous relationship, and an older step-daughter, aged five. We started dating and I helped care for his children whenever they came over to visit. In spite of my fear of relationships, Heng and I went on to get married on 15 August 1980, and I found myself with four children. Then Joe had a one-year-old son, but he divorced and needed help with childcare, so they both came to live with us. Soon I had five youngsters to look after. Life was busy and money was tight. Then the Toxteth riots kicked off less than a year later, in July 1981.

With the economy in recession and unemployment at an all-time high, we decided it was a good time to leave England. Against my better judgement, I returned to Ireland until the riots had died down. I half-expected one of the nuns to knock at my door, but no one came. Then, in 1983, Heng was offered the chance to move to San

Francisco for work. I followed him in July, but was there for only three months before we started to argue and I realised that our marriage was failing. I was 31 years old when I moved back to England in October the same year, but Heng remained out in America. We separated but we didn't get divorced until almost nine years later, in 1992. I was glad to be back on my own again. I realised I'd never be cut out for marriage because I couldn't stand being told what to do. My experience at the hands of the nuns had left me scarred for life.

The following years passed by, and soon I found myself with my girls all grown up. However, the fear of losing them had never really left me. It was only when my first grandchild was born that the fear finally began to diminish. I realised we were a family unit in our own right, and I was the matriarch of that family. For the first time, I felt worthy. Against all odds, I'd managed to raise two daughters and keep them safe, guarding them with my life.

One day, when I was 51 years old, I finally summoned up the courage to call someone – someone whose actions had haunted and changed the course of my life from the beginning – Sister Seraphina. The woman had been on my back my entire life. Now she was one ghost I needed to put to rest. I picked up the phone and dialled a number.

'Is that Sister Seraphina?' I asked, my voice not faltering for a second.

'It is. And who is this calling?' a frail old lady replied on the other end of the line.

'This is Mary Creighton. Do you remember me?'

There was a short pause before she spoke.

'I do.'

'Good. You've managed to control me for years, but I'm calling you now to tell you that you can't control me any longer. You and the others took my children from me, but I'm a mother now, and I'm stronger than you could ever know. So you can take your meddling nose out of my business and feck off!'

I slammed the receiver down in a temper. My entire body was shaking as adrenalin coursed through my veins. I'd done it. I'd finally said what I should have said all those years before. I knew then that I was back on the road to recovery, and that no one would ever use, abuse, or take advantage of me again.

# CHAPTER 23

## Universal Mother

I might have left my past behind, but the torment of having been in those hellholes and the fact I'd had three children taken never once left me. Six years ago, in 2011, I was flicking through some groups on Facebook when one popped up on my profile. I'd already joined a group for the survivors of the Magdalene Laundries when another appeared and made me stop dead in my tracks. It was called the Banished Babies, and it was a collection of children who had been taken or adopted from mother-and-baby units across Ireland, including Castlepollard, and farmed out to America. I contacted one of my Facebook friends from the Magdalene Laundry group and told her I'd also been in Castlepollard.

'I often think of those children – all those babies taken from their mothers – but I was luckier than most because friends "bought" me my freedom, so I was able to leave with my child. But the nuns were always on my back, even though I'd got out. Afterwards, my life was never my own.'

I explained about the 'cornflake babies', and the thousands of passport photos I'd found the day I'd looked inside the cupboard under the stairs.

'I'm certain all those little mites had been farmed out, most likely to America. Rich couples would "buy" babies and take them back home. It was a scandal of the highest order – babies being "sold" like cattle.'

My friend asked me if there were any children in particular that I remembered.

'Two little boys,' I told her. 'One was the baby of my friend Kerry, who saved my life after we ran away together; the other was my best friend Caitlin's baby. Their faces will never leave me.'

Then my friend had some news for me: 'There's someone in the group, I think you might know him because his mother was there at the same time as you.'

I gasped as she described the man he had become and the baby he had been.

'He had the bluest eyes I've ever seen,' she remarked.

My heart missed a beat because I knew in that moment it was Aiden, Caitlin's son.

'Don't tell me his name, because I can tell you everything about him, including his mother's address in Ireland.'

And I did.

'That's him, that's the same baby,' she gasped.

'Can you put me in touch with him?'

'I can do better than that; you can join the Facebook group.'

So I did. I introduced myself to the rest of the group, explaining that although I wasn't a Castlepollard baby,

I was a mother looking for her own 'stolen' children. I wasn't sure if I'd be accepted, but I was, and with open arms. Aiden and I soon made contact. He told me he'd been adopted by a couple in Ireland, but that Caitlin had gone on to marry his biological father and they had more children together. I was happy for Caitlin, but saddened that she had to lose her eldest child in order to pick up the same life before going into Castlepollard. Then Aiden told me something even more chilling. Although Caitlin had remembered Aiden, she'd blocked out her entire time at Castlepollard. It had seemed the trauma of having her baby boy ripped from her arms had wiped out everything. It must have been a kind of post-traumatic stress – the brain's way of coping with such an emotional trauma.

'What? She remembers nothing?' I gasped.

'No,' Aiden replied.

The thought that Caitlin had suffered such a trauma, yet had managed to find her lost son spurred me to find my own girls.

Then I heard Kerry's story through the wife of Peter, the beautiful baby boy with a head of golden curls. His mother had been a respectable woman who had given birth to several beautiful children inside Castlepollard. Although she'd been married, the Church, in its wisdom, decided she couldn't cope with motherhood and so 'farmed' out several of her babies. Against all odds, Kerry's children – apart from one – eventually found one another and together they traced their wonderful mother. But Peter's wife hadn't finished.

'Kerry died only a month to the day after her children had found her. It's so sad.'

It was. Both women had suffered so much, but Kerry more than the others because she'd had four children taken.

After joining the group, lots of the banished babies from the Castlepollard Mother-and-Baby Home group asked me questions such as: *Did I know their mother? Or what was it really like inside one of the mother-and-baby units in Ireland?*

I told them the truth, and they in turn accepted me without judgement. One day, one of the banished babies sent me a private message over Facebook. In it, he called me the Universal Mother – a symbol of hope for all the babies searching for their own mothers.

'We've waited a long time for you to come along, Mary. We need you to give us answers to some of our questions.'

Unintentionally, I'd become a symbol of everything they'd lost. I'd unwittingly become a positive focal point for those lost children who hadn't managed to find their own mothers. I discovered many of these 'babies', now grown adults, had suffered problems with their digestive systems, yet none of them knew why.

'It was the porridge,' I told them. 'The nuns made us force-feed our babies porridge at just six weeks old. It was horrible,' I said, as I recounted the plastic sheet on the floor and the constant stream of projectile vomit and the pitiful cries that had reduced us all to tears.

The nuns had treated us no better than animals, and now our children were paying for our so-called 'sins'.

I'd joined a group fighting for justice for the survivors of the Magdalene Laundries.

'Put my name down,' I told them. 'I was in one of them, and I'll help in any way I can.'

However, on 6 February 2014, the authorities in Ireland, dealing with the compensation claims, wrote to me, denying I was ever at High Park in Dublin.

'We have no record of you being there,' it read.

I called them up.

'But I was there for 77 days,' I insisted. 'And I remember each and every day I spent there.'

'It doesn't matter. There's no official record of you ever having been there.'

I was momentarily flummoxed. I'd been due to go to Dunboyne, but Sister Celestine and Mrs Elroy, the social worker, had dropped me off at High Park and left me to my own fate.

*But with no documentation, how could I prove it all these years later? Even if I could, who would believe the word of a so-called 'fallen woman' over that of a priest or nun?*

I was stumped. Although I was delighted that others were able to prove they were there and get compensation

– belated rightful pay for the work they did inside that sweatshop – I could not. Not long afterwards, I was sat doodling at the dining room table when my grandson asked me what I was doing.

'I'm drawing a picture of a place where I was once held against my will,' I explained, as my blue biro scrawled across the page to form a childlike drawing.

'So it's still hurting you, Grandma?' he asked, looking up at me from the sofa.

'Yes, son.'

My grandson scratched his head and thought for a moment, and then he spoke.

'But if you can remember it so well that you can draw it then you still have it in here,' he said, pointing towards his head. 'This trauma.'

And that's when I had a light-bulb moment. He was right: if I could recall High Park in so much detail that I was able to draw it, how could they deny I'd been there? Especially when I could draw and describe every door, every bed, and every window?

I walked over to my grandson and planted a kiss on his head.

'What was that for?' he asked, a little confused.

'That's for being a clever boy.'

I took the piece of paper, wrote a covering letter, and posted it off first-class to Dublin, Ireland, where I asked the powers that be to check my drawing against one of the blueprints of High Park.

*If I never stayed there, then how could I draw such an accurate sketch of the inside of the Magdalene Laundry?*

Five days later, a letter landed on my doormat at home. It was postmarked from Ireland.

'*I wish to confirm that you were resident from 28 March to 13 June 1974,*' it read.

Another letter said it had found correspondence from the Western Health Board that had referred to me. It had been written by Mrs Elroy, the social worker. On the back of it was a handwritten note, confirming my stay at the Magdalene Laundry. The authorities agreed to take it as proof of my residency there, but I know it was because I'd shamed them and could recall even the smallest details of my surroundings at High Park. I was later awarded 11,500 euros – around £10,000 – for my imprisonment, but no amount of money could compensate me for the time I'd spent inside that place. We'd been treated like dogs, but now people were slowly waking up to what had happened all those years ago. People had started to question the Catholic Church and its dealings with the poor unmarried mothers of Ireland – the ones who survived, that is.

More things started to come to light, unimaginable things. In 1993, the nuns, who had been dabbling on the Stock Exchange, lost money after one of the companies they'd invested in went bust. To cover the loss they decided to sell a portion of their land at a convent in Dublin to a property developer. The only problem was the land – High Park laundry – contained a mass grave.

The Sisters of Our Lady of Charity settled on a deal with the developer to split the costs of clearing the grave. This included exhuming and cremating the bodies and placing the ashes in another mass grave in Glasnevin Cemetery. But there was another problem: when the bodies were exhumed, they discovered 22 more than they had listed. In fact, over one third of the deaths had never been certified, and the nuns didn't even know the names of some of the women. In the end, a total of 155 bodies were exhumed and cremated. All these women had died in the service of the nuns.

As if that wasn't shocking enough, even more came to light, including a mass grave discovered at a former Catholic home for women in Bon Secours Mother-and-Baby home, in Tuam, County Galway. Initial reports stated that there could be as many as 800 babies' bodies found, ranging in age from just 35 weeks to three years old. Most had been buried in the 1950s. An inquiry had been launched after local historian, Catherine Corless, said there was evidence of an unmarked grave at the home, where records showed almost 800 children had died between 1925 and 1961. However, there was a burial record for just one child. Ms Corless also said that nine mothers had died in the home during its existence.

In 2014, the Archbishop of Dublin was reported to have said that 'if something happened in Tuam, it probably happened in other mother-and-baby homes around the country.'

In March 2017, it was reported that Tuam was the tip of the iceberg when it came to deaths. The Bon Secours Mother-and-Baby Home in Tuam is just one of 14 mother-and-baby homes now being investigated by The Commission of Investigation. A judicial commission of investigation, established in February 2015 by an order of the Irish government, it was set up in the wake of the mass grave found at Tuam. It is investigating the records of and practices at 13 additional mother-and-baby homes as well as Tuam. The Commission will examine the experiences of women and children who lived in mother-and-baby homes over the period 1922–1998. This includes their living conditions, mortality rates, post-mortem practices, reporting and burial arrangements, among many other things. The Commission is due to publish a report into its findings in February next year (2018), which will then be passed on to the Minister for Children.

Whatever the findings, it appears there was abuse and exploitation of pregnant women and girls on an industrial scale across Ireland, not to mention the poor babies born inside those homes – the last of which closed in 1996. Approximately 35,000 women and girls went through nine mother-and-baby homes (and a small number of associated institutions operated by various religious orders on behalf of the state) between 1904 and 1996. It is understood that around 6,000 babies and children died, and their births and deaths were registered.

At Castlepollard, it's believed that approximately 4,000 women and girls passed through the doors over the years it was a mother-and-baby home. New research by the Castlepollard group of survivors has found 200 confirmed and registered deaths of babies and children buried in the 'Angel's Plot', ranging from just a few hours old to over two years. There were also 77 confirmed still-births. Castlepollard was one of three homes run by the Order of the Sacred Heart. Invited over from England in 1922, the Order first bought a 200-acre farm in Bessborough, County Cork, to deal with the problem of unmarried mothers. It later bought a second home which they renamed Sean Ross Abbey. In the early 1930s, it built St Peters – a three-storey, 120-bed maternity hospital – later known as Castlepollard. Over the years, the nuns never employed a doctor or even nurses, only one midwife – Nurse Smith while I was there – at a time. This was the absolute minimum required by law. The local authority paid the nuns a weekly 'Capitation Grant' from the county where the girl had come from. It was said to be 16 shillings per mother, per week, and £1 and 2 shillings and 6 pence per baby or child. The nuns didn't waste money on luxuries such as medical equipment, painkillers, or, as I knew from bitter experience from working in the nursery, nappy rash cream, unless it was absolutely necessary.

Also, in March 2017, survivors from Castlepollard released hundreds of names of everyone known to have died there. I discovered that around 3,763 babies had been born at Castlepollard and had had their births registered. There were 203 registered deaths. However, some ledgers are either missing or did not exist, so the true figure may never be known, but is thought to be somewhere between 400 and 500. The Castlepollard babies are buried in a small Angel's Plot down a lane around a quarter of a mile from the main manor house. Even more chilling is that local people have testified that workmen tending the grounds hammered a horseshoe nail into a perimeter wall every time a baby was laid to rest in the graveyard. The workmen, it seemed, had shown those babies and children more respect than the nuns, marking out each lost life in some small way. At least they had the decency to do that and also provide clues as to just how many babies have been buried there. I thought back to the banging noise I'd heard while I was in Castlepollard, and my blood ran cold. Every time I heard a hammer bang, it was probably to signify another death, another young life snuffed out before it had even begun.

Today, that same wall is said to have over 100 nails in it. Along the wall, approximately 12 to 18 inches apart, and standing over 3 foot from the ground with some higher and others lower, is a plethora of horseshoe nails. The nails are thought to be makeshift headstones of where the baby or child was buried, and they are everywhere. Time and overgrown ivy has covered and concealed many of them, but we, their mothers, will

# Afterword

It took me years, but, supported by my two daughters, Charlotte and Elizabeth, I finally traced my eldest daughter, Catherine. She had been adopted by a family, and we briefly made contact. However, it was short-lived. Sadly, she then axed contact and I have not heard from her again. My second child, who was taken by social services at the same time as her sister, I lost all contact with. My search for her continues. My third child, who I called Zada, was difficult to trace. But a friend of mine, living in Ireland, gave me a copy of her birth certificate on my 60th birthday, five years ago. To my horror, I discovered that when I'd signed it in the hospital, I'd actually signed a certificate without the name Zada on it. I recalled how the woman had repeatedly asked me to spell out the name, which I did. But it transpired I'd been tricked again, because not only had she omitted the name Zada from the birth certificate, she'd actually changed it completely, choosing a name – Rochelle – of her own liking. I'd asked her at the time to let me read the certificate, but the woman had been reluctant. Now I knew why. If nothing else, it would be a foolproof way of ensuring I was never able to trace the third and final baby they had taken from me.

In spite of everything I've been through I still believe in God, I just don't believe in religion. My hatred of nuns remains to this day, because if they had stayed away from me then maybe I'd still be in contact with all my children now. They took three of my children away from me, and if they hadn't got involved in the first place then social services wouldn't have been on my back. But once you've been labelled, it seems that everyone uses the exact same brush to tarnish you even more.

My dear father later developed emphysema as a result of a lifetime smoking habit, and he died in Liverpool on 15 July 1992. My mother lived another nine years, but in spite what she'd done to me as a child, I cared for her because she was my mother. When she suffered a series of debilitating strokes I nursed her during the last few years of her life right up until her death on 11 January 2001. I didn't wish her any ill. In her mind, she was just doing what she thought was best and what the nuns had advised her to do.

For the best part of 50 years I remained silent, ashamed of what had happened to me, but I refuse to be silenced any more. The shame lies with the Catholic Church and the cover-ups it orchestrated to try and hide what was really happening behind the closed doors of these so-called 'caring' institutions. Inquiries and compensation will not bring back those poor lost souls – the mothers who died during childbirth, or the poor babies and children buried in shoeboxes in the cold, hard earth. But at least by speaking out they can and will be remembered. They did exist and they did matter. They still do, and they always will.

# Acknowledgements

I'd like to start by thanking my daughters, whom I all love dearly. Thank you for always being there for me each and every step of the way.

To Mr and Mrs Campbell and their family, who supported me from day one of this nightmare journey. Their kindness knew no bounds.

To Mary Crawley, who was both my friend and confidante. You were always there for me when I needed you, Mary, and I love you from the bottom of my heart. I'm just sad that you are no longer here on this earth to see that I have finally managed to put all this down in book form.

My gratitude must also go to Barbara, a dear friend. She not only encouraged me, but put me in contact with both her, and now my, ghost writer, Veronica Clark, who helped me write and put this whole book together. Thank you, Barbara, you mean an awful lot to me, and thank you, Veronica, for being my 'voice'. Thank you also to my agent, Eve White, and to Kelly at Blink Publishing, for believing in my story.

Last, but not least, to Ina in Edinburgh, who was and will always be one of my dearest friends. I love you, Ina.

I'd also like to pay tribute to all those mothers and babies who lost their lives during the scandal of the Magdalene laundries and the countless wicked mother-and-baby homes. The word 'Magdalen' actually means sinner, but we weren't sinners: we were just young girls trying to find our way in a society that supposedly prided itself on family values. Yet, in an astonishing case of double standards, thousands of women and children were locked away, hidden from view, and shipped out. It was, and will always be, Ireland's greatest shame.